MEDIA AND COMMUNICATIONS - TECHNOLOGIES,
POLICIES AND CHALLENGES

SOCIAL MEDIA
USE IN THE FEDERAL
GOVERNMENT

MEDIA AND COMMUNICATIONS-
TECHNOLOGIES,
POLICIES AND CHALLENGES

MEDIA AND COMMUNICATIONS - TECHNOLOGIES,
POLICIES AND CHALLENGES

SOCIAL MEDIA USE IN THE FEDERAL GOVERNMENT

Michael N. Brander
EDITOR

Nova Science Publishers, Inc.
New York

NOTICE TO THE READER

The Publisher has taken reasonable care in the preparation of this book, but makes no expressed or implied warranty of any kind and assumes no responsibility for any errors or omissions. No liability is assumed for incidental or consequential damages in connection with or arising out of information contained in this book. The Publisher shall not be liable for any special, consequential, or exemplary damages resulting, in whole or in part, from the readers' use of, or reliance upon, this material. Any parts of this book based on government reports are so indicated and copyright is claimed for those parts to the extent applicable to compilations of such works.

Independent verification should be sought for any data, advice or recommendations contained in this book. In addition, no responsibility is assumed by the publisher for any injury and/or damage to persons or property arising from any methods, products, instructions, ideas or otherwise contained in this publication.

This publication is designed to provide accurate and authoritative information with regard to the subject matter covered herein. It is sold with the clear understanding that the Publisher is not engaged in rendering legal or any other professional services. If legal or any other expert assistance is required, the services of a competent person should be sought. FROM A DECLARATION OF PARTICIPANTS JOINTLY ADOPTED BY A COMMITTEE OF THE AMERICAN BAR ASSOCIATION AND A COMMITTEE OF PUBLISHERS.

Additional color graphics may be available in the e-book version of this book.

Library of Congress Cataloging-in-Publication Data

Social media use in the federal government / editor, Michael N. Brander.
p. cm.
Includes index.
ISBN 978-1-62100-747-0 (softcover)
1. Administrative agencies--Information technology--United States. 2. Electronic government information--United States--Management. 3. Administrative agencies--United States--Management--Technological innovations. 4. United States. Congress--Constituent communication--Technological innovations. I. Brander, Michael N.
JK468.A8S63 2012
352.3'802854678--dc23
2011038568

Published by Nova Science Publishers, Inc. † New York

CONTENTS

PREFACE

Beginning with the widespread use of e-mail by Congress in the mid-1990's, the development of new electronic technologies has altered the traditional patterns of communication between Members of Congress and constituents. Many Members now use e-mail, official websites, blogs, YouTube channels, and Facebook pages to communicate with their constituents—technologies that were either non-existent or not widely available 15 years ago. The use of these social media services, including popular Web sites like Facebook, Twitter, and YouTube, has been endorsed by President Obama and provides opportunities for agencies to more readily share information with and solicit feedback from the public. However, these services may also pose risks to the adequate protection of both personal and government information.

Chapter 1- Federal agencies increasingly use recently developed Internet technologies that allow individuals or groups to create, organize, comment on, and share online content. The use of these social media services—including popular Web sites like Facebook, Twitter, and YouTube—has been endorsed by President Obama and provides opportunities for agencies to more readily share information with and solicit feedback from the public. However, these services may also pose risks to the adequate protection of both personal and government information.

GAO was asked to (1) describe how federal agencies are currently using commercially provided social media services and (2) determine the extent to which agencies have developed and implemented policies and procedures for managing and protecting information associated with this use. To do this, GAO examined the headquarters-level Facebook pages, Twitter accounts, and YouTube channels of 24 major federal agencies; reviewed pertinent policies, procedures, and guidance; and interviewed officials involved in agency use of social media.

Chapter 2- "Web 2.0" technologies—such as Web logs ("blogs"), social networking Web sites, video- and multimedia-sharing sites, and "wikis"—are increasingly being utilized by federal agencies to communicate with the public. These tools have the potential to, among other things, better include the public in the governing process. However, agency use of these technologies can present risks associated with properly managing and protecting government records and sensitive information, including personally identifiable information. In light of the rapidly increasing popularity of Web 2.0 technologies, GAO was asked to identify and describe current uses of Web 2.0 technologies by federal agencies and key challenges associated with their use.

To accomplish this, GAO analyzed federal policies, reports, and guidance related to the use of Web 2.0 technologies and interviewed officials at selected federal agencies, including the Department of Homeland Security, the General Services Administration, and the National Archives and Records Administration.

Chapter 3- Beginning with the widespread use of e-mail by Congress in the mid-1990's, the development of new electronic technologies has altered the traditional patterns of communication between Members of Congress and constituents. Many Members now use e-mail, official websites, blogs, YouTube channels, and Facebook pages to communicate with their constituents—technologies that were either non-existent or not widely available 15 years ago.

These technologies have arguably served to enhance the ability of Members of Congress to fulfill their representational duties by providing greater opportunities for communication between the Member and individual constituents, supporting the fundamental democratic role of spreading information about public policy and government operations. In addition, electronic technology has reduced the marginal cost of constituent communications; unlike postal letters, Members can reach large numbers of constituents for a relatively small fixed cost. Despite these advantages, electronic communications have raised some concerns. Existing law and chamber regulations on the use of communication media such as the franking privilege have proven difficult to adapt to the new electronic technologies.

In: Social Media ...
Editor: Michael N. Brander

ISBN: 978-1-62100-747-0
© 2012 Nova Science Publishers, Inc.

Chapter 1

SOCIAL MEDIA: FEDERAL AGENCIES NEED POLICIES AND PROCEDURES FOR MANAGING AND PROTECTING INFORMATION THEY ACCESS AND DISSEMINATE[*]

United States Government Accountability Office

WHY GAO DID THIS STUDY

Federal agencies increasingly use recently developed Internet technologies that allow individuals or groups to create, organize, comment on, and share online content. The use of these social media services—including popular Web sites like Facebook, Twitter, and YouTube—has been endorsed by President Obama and provides opportunities for agencies to more readily share information with and solicit feedback from the public. However, these services may also pose risks to the adequate protection of both personal and government information.

---

[*] This is an edited, reformatted and augmented version of a United States Government Accountability Office Report GAO-11-605 dated June, 2011.

GAO was asked to (1) describe how federal agencies are currently using commercially provided social media services and (2) determine the extent to which agencies have developed and implemented policies and procedures for managing and protecting information associated with this use. To do this, GAO examined the headquarters-level Facebook pages, Twitter accounts, and YouTube channels of 24 major federal agencies; reviewed pertinent policies, procedures, and guidance; and interviewed officials involved in agency use of social media.

WHAT GAO RECOMMENDS

GAO recommends that agencies ensure that appropriate records management, privacy, and security measures are in place. Most of the agencies agreed with GAO's recommendations. Three agencies did not agree with recommendations made to them; GAO maintains that the actions are necessary.

WHAT GAO FOUND

Federal agencies have been adapting commercially provided social media technologies to support their missions. Specifically, GAO identified several distinct ways that 23 of 24 major agencies are using Facebook, Twitter, and YouTube. These include reposting information available on official agency Web sites, posting information not otherwise available on agency Web sites, soliciting comments from the public, responding to comments on posted content, and providing links to non-government sites. For example, agencies used Facebook to post pictures or descriptions of the activities of agency officials and to interact with the public. Agencies used Twitter to provide information in an abbreviated format and to direct the public back to official agency sites. YouTube was used to provide alternate means of accessing videos available on official agency sites, share videos of agency officials discussing topics of interest, or to solicit feedback from the public.

The use of these services can pose challenges in managing and identifying records, protecting personal information, and ensuring the security of federal information and systems. However, the 23 major agencies that GAO identified as using social media have made mixed progress in developing and implementing policies and procedures to address these challenges:

- **Records management:** 12 of the 23 agencies have developed and issued guidance that outlines processes and policies for identifying and managing records generated by their use of social media and record-keeping roles and responsibilities.
- **Privacy:** 12 agencies have updated their privacy policies to describe whether they use personal information made available through social media, and 8 conducted and documented privacy impact assessments to identify potential privacy risks that may exist in using social media given the likelihood that personal information will be made available to the agency by the public.
- **Security:** 7 agencies identified and documented security risks (such as the potential for an attacker to use social media to collect information and launch attacks against federal information systems) and mitigating controls associated with their use of social media.

In several cases, agencies reported having policies in development to address these issues. In other cases, agencies reported that there was no need to have policies or procedures that specifically address the use of social media, since these are addressed in existing policies. However, social media technologies present unique challenges and risks, and without establishing guidance and assessing risks specific to social media, agencies cannot be assured that they are adequately meeting their responsibilities to manage and preserve federal records, protect the privacy of personal information, and secure federal systems and information against threats.

ABBREVIATIONS

CIO	Chief Information Officer
DHS	Department of Homeland Security
DOD	Department of Defense
DOE	Department of Energy
FISMA	Federal Information Security Management Act
FTC	Federal Trade Commission
HUD	Department of Housing and Urban Development
NARA	National Archives and Records Administration

NASA	National Aeronautics and Space Administration
NIST	National Institute of Standards and Technology
NRC	Nuclear Regulatory Commission
OMB	Office of Management and Budget
PIA	privacy impact assessment
PII	personally identifiable information
SBA	Small Business Administration
SSA	Social Security Administration

June 28, 2011

Congressional Requesters:

Federal agencies are increasingly using recently developed Internet technologies (commonly referred to as "Web 2.0" technologies) that offer flexible, sophisticated capabilities for interaction with individuals, allowing participants to publish comments, photos, and videos directly on agency-sponsored Web pages. These technologies include services offered by social networking sites (such as Facebook and Twitter) and video-sharing Web sites (such as YouTube), which allow individuals or groups of individuals to create, organize, edit, comment on, and share content.

The use of these services by federal agencies was endorsed in a January 2009 memorandum by President Obama promoting transparency and open government.[1] The memorandum encouraged executive departments and agencies to harness new technologies to put information about their operations and decisions online so that it would be readily available to the public. It also encouraged the solicitation of public feedback to identify information of the greatest use to the public, assess and improve levels of collaboration, and identify new opportunities for cooperation in government. However, while such use of social media offers the potential to better include people in the governing process and further agency missions, use of these services may also pose risks that government records and sensitive information, including personally identifiable information (PII),[2] is not properly managed or protected.

You asked us to review federal agencies' use of commercially provided social media services. Specifically, as agreed with your offices, our objectives were to (1) describe how federal agencies are currently using commercially provided social media services, and (2) determine the extent to which federal agencies have developed and implemented policies and procedures for managing and protecting information associated with this use.

To address our first objective, we examined department-level Facebook pages, Twitter accounts, and YouTube channels associated with each of the 24 major federal agencies covered by the Chief Financial Officers Act[3] to describe the types of information agencies disseminated via the services and the nature of their interactions with the public.[4] We categorized agency use based on types of information found on their social media pages.[5] In addition, we interviewed agency officials to discuss the extent to which they collect and use personally identifiable information provided by the public on their social media pages.

To address our second objective, we reviewed pertinent records management, privacy, and security policies, procedures, guidance, and risk assessments in place at each of the 23 major agencies and compared them to relevant federal regulations and guidance on records management, privacy, and security. We also reviewed relevant reports and studies to identify records management, privacy, and security risks associated with social media use by federal agencies. Finally, in coordination with the National Academy of Public Administration,[6] we conducted a roundtable discussion to solicit views on these issues from federal officials involved in agency use of social media.

We conducted this performance audit from July 2010 to June 2011 in accordance with generally accepted government auditing standards. Those standards require that we plan and perform the audit to obtain sufficient, appropriate evidence to provide a reasonable basis for our findings and conclusions based on our audit objectives. We believe that the evidence obtained provides a reasonable basis for our findings and conclusions based on our audit objectives. Our objectives, scope, and methodology are discussed in more detail in appendix I.

BACKGROUND

Internet-based services using Web 2.0 technology have become increasingly popular. Web 2.0 technologies are a second generation of the World Wide Web as an enabling platform for Web-based communities of interest, collaboration, and interactive services. These technologies include Web logs (known as "blogs"), which allow individuals to respond online to agency notices and other postings; "wikis," which allow individual users to directly collaborate on the content of Web pages; "podcasting," which allows users to download audio content; and "mashups," which are Web sites that combine content from multiple sources. Web 2.0 technologies also include social media services, which allow individuals or groups of individuals to create, organize, edit, comment on, and share content. These include social networking sites (such as Facebook and Twitter) and video-sharing Web sites (such as YouTube).

While in the past Internet usage concentrated on sites that provide online shopping opportunities and other services, according to the Nielsen Company,[7] social media-related sites have moved to the forefront. In June 2010, it reported that Internet users worldwide accessed social media sites one out of every 4 1/2 minutes they spent online on average. The use of social networking services now reportedly exceeds Web-based e-mail usage, and the number of American users frequenting online video sites has more than tripled since 2003. The Nielsen Company reported that during the month of April 2010, the average user spent nearly 6 hours on social media-related sites.

Facebook is a social networking site that lets users create personal profiles describing themselves and then locate and connect with friends, co-workers, and others who share similar interests or who have common backgrounds. Individual profiles may contain—at the user's discretion—detailed personal information, including birth date, home address, telephone number, employment history, educational background, and religious beliefs. Facebook also allows any user to establish a "page" to represent an organization (including federal agencies), business, or public figure in order to disseminate information to users who choose to connect with them. These users can leave comments in response to information posted on such a page. Profile information for these users may be made available to the administrators of these pages, depending on settings controlled by the user. According to the Facebook site, Facebook has over 500 million active users who spend more than 700 billion minutes per month on Facebook.

Twitter is a social networking site that allows users to share and receive information through short messages that are also known as "tweets." These messages are no longer than 140 characters in length. Twitter users can establish accounts by providing a limited amount of PII but may elect to provide additional PII if they wish. Users can post messages to their profile pages and reply to other Twitter users' tweets. Users can "follow" other users as well—i.e., subscribe to their tweets. In March 2011, Twitter reported adding an average of 460,000 new accounts and facilitating the delivery of 140 million tweets every day.

YouTube is a video-sharing site that allows users to discover, watch, upload, comment on, and share originally created videos. Similar to Twitter, users can establish accounts on YouTube with only limited amounts of PII, although they may choose to provide more detailed information on their profile page. Users can comment on videos posted on a page either in written responses or by uploading their own videos.[8] According to YouTube, during 2010 more than 13 million hours of video were uploaded.

Federal agencies are increasingly using these social media tools to enhance services and interactions with the public. As of April 2011, 23 of 24 major federal agencies had established accounts on Facebook, Twitter, and YouTube.[9] Furthermore, the public increasingly follows the information provided by federal agencies on these services. For example, as of April 2011, the U.S. Department of State had over 72,000 users following its Facebook page; the National Aeronautics and Space Administration (NASA) had over 992,000 Twitter followers; and a video uploaded by NASA on YouTube in December 2010 had over 360,000 views as of April 2011.

Federal Agencies Are Responsible for Managing Records, Protecting Privacy, and Ensuring Adequate Security

The Federal Records Act establishes requirements for records management programs in federal agencies. Each federal agency is required to make and preserve records that (1) document the organization, functions, policies, decisions, procedures, and essential transactions of the agency and (2) provide the information necessary to protect the legal and financial rights of the government and of persons directly affected by the agency's activities. The Federal Records Act defines a federal record without respect to format. Records include all books, papers, maps, photographs, machine readable materials, or other documentary materials, regardless of physical form or characteristics, made or received by an agency of the government under federal law or in connection with the transaction of public business and preserved or appropriate for preservation by that agency as evidence of the organization, functions, policies, decisions, procedures, operations, or other activities of the government or because of the informational value of data in them.

The agency responsible for providing guidance for adhering to the Federal Records Act is the National Archives and Records Administration (NARA). NARA is responsible for issuing records management guidance; working with agencies to implement effective controls over the creation, maintenance, and use of records in the conduct of agency business; providing oversight of agencies' records management programs; approving the disposition (destruction or preservation) of records; and providing storage facilities for agency records.

In October 2010, NARA issued a bulletin to provide guidance to federal agencies in managing records produced when federal agencies use social media platforms for federal business.[10] The bulletin highlighted the requirement for agencies to decide how they will manage records created in social media environments in accordance with applicable federal laws and regulations. As part of this effort, the guidance emphasized the need for active participation of agency records management staff, Web managers, social media managers, information technology staff, privacy and information security staff, and other relevant stakeholders at each federal agency.

Privacy Laws and Guidance Set Requirements to Ensure the Protection of Personal Information

The primary laws that provide privacy protections for personal information accessed or held by the federal government are the Privacy Act of 1974 and E-Government Act of 2002. These laws describe, among other things, agency responsibilities with regard to protecting PII. The Privacy Act places limitations on agencies' collection, disclosure, and use of personal information maintained in systems of records. A system of records is a collection of information about individuals under control of an agency from which information is retrieved by the name of an individual or other identifier. The E-Government Act of 2002 requires agencies to assess the impact of federal information systems on individuals' privacy. Specifically, the E-Government Act strives to enhance the protection of personal information in government information systems and information collections by requiring agencies to conduct privacy impact assessments (PIA).

A PIA is an analysis of how personal information is collected, stored, shared, and managed in a federal system. Specifically, according to Office of Management and Budget (OMB) guidance, the purpose of a PIA is to (1) ensure handling conforms to applicable legal, regulatory, and policy requirements regarding privacy; (2) determine the risks and effects of collecting, maintaining, and disseminating information in identifiable form in an electronic information system; and (3) examine and evaluate protections and alternative processes for handling information to mitigate potential privacy risks.

In June 2010, OMB issued guidance to federal agencies for protecting privacy when using Web-based technologies (such as social media).[11] The guidance built upon the protections and requirements outlined in the Privacy Act and E-Government Act and called for agencies to develop transparent privacy policies and notices to ensure that agencies provide adequate notice of their use of social media services to the public, and to analyze privacy implications whenever federal agencies choose to use such technologies to engage with the public.

Key Laws and Guidance Set Agencies' Responsibilities for Securing Government Information

The Federal Information Security Management Act of 2002 (FISMA) established a framework designed to ensure the effectiveness of security controls over information resources that support federal operations and assets. According to FISMA, each agency is responsible for, among other things, providing information security protections commensurate with the risk and magnitude of the harm resulting from unauthorized access, use, disclosure, disruption, modification, or destruction of information collected or maintained by or on behalf of the agency and information systems used or operated by an agency or by a contractor of an agency or other organization on behalf of an agency.

Consistent with its statutory responsibilities under FISMA, in August 2009 the National Institute of Standards and Technology (NIST) issued an update to its guidance on recommended security controls for federal information systems and organizations.[12] The NIST guidance directs agencies to select and specify security controls for information systems based on an assessment of the risk to organizational operations and assets, individuals, other organizations, and the nation associated with operation of those systems. According to the guidance, the use of a risk-based approach is applicable not just to the operation of the agency's internal systems but is also important when an agency is using technology for which its ability to establish security controls may be limited, such as when using a third-party social media service.

GAO Has Identified Challenges in Agencies' Use of Social Media

In July 2010, we testified that while the use of Web 2.0 technologies, including social media technologies, can transform how federal agencies engage the public by allowing citizens to be more involved in the governing process, agency use of such technologies can also present challenges related to records management, privacy, and security.[13]

- **Records Management:** We reported that Web 2.0 technologies raised issues concerning the government's ability to identify and preserve federal records. Agencies may face challenges in assessing whether the information they generate and receive by means of these technologies constitutes federal records. Furthermore, once the need to preserve information as federal records has been established, mechanisms need to be put in place to capture such records and preserve them properly. We stated that proper records retention management needs to take into account NARA record scheduling requirements and federal law, which require that the disposition of all federal records be planned according to an agency schedule or a general records schedule approved by NARA.

    We highlighted that these requirements may be challenging for agencies because the types of records involved when information is collected via Web 2.0 technologies may not be clear. As previously mentioned, in October 2010, NARA issued further guidance that clarified agency responsibilities in making records determinations.

- **Privacy:** We noted, among other things, that agencies faced challenges in ensuring that they are taking appropriate steps to limit the collection and use of personal information made available through social media. We stated that privacy could be compromised if clear limits were not set on how the government uses personal information to which it has access in social networking environments. Social networking sites, such as Facebook, encourage people to provide personal information that they intend to be used only for social purposes. Government agencies that participate in such sites may have access to this information and may need rules on how such information can be used. While such agencies cannot control what information may be captured by social networking sites, they can make determinations about what information they will collect and what to disclose. However, unless rules to guide their decisions are clear, agencies could handle information inconsistently. OMB's subsequent release of guidance, as previously discussed, clarified agency requirements for such privacy protections.

- **Security:** We highlighted that federal government information systems have been targeted by persistent, pervasive, and aggressive threats and that, as a result, personal and agency information needs to be safeguarded from security threats, and that guidance may be needed for employees on how to use social media Web sites properly and how to handle information in the context of social media.

Table 1. Examples of Security Threats Agencies Face When Using Commercially Provided Social Media Services

Social media threat	Description
Spear phishing	An attack targeting a specific user or group of users that attempts to deceive the user into performing an action, such as opening a document or clicking a link, that can lead to a compromise of the user's system by installing malicious software. Spear phishers rely on knowing personal information about their target, such as an event, interest, travel plans, or current issues, that allows them to gain the confidence of their victims. Sometimes this information is gathered by hacking into the targeted network, but often it is easy to look up personal details about target victims on a social media network.
Social engineering	An attack using personal information to build trust with a user in order to gain unauthorized access to sensitive information, systems, and networks or to engage in identity fraud, among other things. For example, an attacker may learn personal information about an individual through a social media service and build a trust relationship by expressing interest in similar topics. Once the victim trusts the attacker, the attacker can collect additional information about the user or use their relationship to expand the attacker's influence to other users and friends, further compromising networks and systems and jeopardizing additional individuals.
Web application attack	An attack utilizing custom Web applications embedded within social media sites, which can lead to installation of malicious code onto federal computers to be used to gain unauthorized access. A hijacked account of a federal user or a federal account may allow for unauthorized posts, tweets, or messages to be seen by the public as official messages, or may be used to spread malicious software by encouraging users to click links or download unwanted applications.

Source: GAO analysis of CIO Council data.

Cyber attacks continue to pose a potentially devastating threat to the systems and operations of the federal government. In February 2011, the Director of National Intelligence testified that, in the previous year, there had been a dramatic increase in malicious cyber activity targeting U.S. computers and networks, including a more than tripling of the volume of malicious software since 2009.[14]

Further, in March 2011, the Federal Trade Commission (FTC) reached an agreement with Twitter to resolve charges that the company deceived consumers and put their privacy at risk by failing to safeguard their personal information. The FTC alleged that serious lapses in the company's security allowed hackers to obtain unauthorized administrative control of Twitter and send unauthorized tweets from user accounts, including one tweet, purportedly from President Obama, that offered his more than 150,000 "followers" a chance to win $500 in free gasoline, in exchange for filling out a survey. To resolve the charges, Twitter agreed to establish and maintain a comprehensive information security program that would be assessed by an independent auditor every other year for 10 years.[15]

According to a Chief Information Officers (CIO) Council report released in September 2009, as the federal government begins to utilize public social media Web sites, advanced persistent threats may be targeted against these Web sites. In addition, attackers may use social media to collect information and launch attacks against federal information systems. Table 1 summarizes three types of security threats identified by the CIO Council that agencies may face when using commercially provided social media services.

The rapid development of social media technologies makes it challenging to keep up with the constantly evolving threats deployed against them and raises the risks associated with government participation in such technologies.

FEDERAL AGENCIES HAVE USED SOCIAL MEDIA SERVICES FOR A VARIETY OF PURPOSES

Federal agencies have been using social media services to support their individual missions. While Facebook, Twitter, and YouTube offer unique ways for agencies to interact with the public, we identified several distinct ways that federal agencies are using the three social media services. Despite varying features of the three platforms, agency interactions can be broadly categorized by the manner in which information is exchanged with the public, including reposting information already available on an agency Web site, posting original content not available on agency Web sites, soliciting feedback from the public, responding to comments, and linking to non-government Web sites. Figure 1 shows how the 23 agencies[16] use each of these functions.

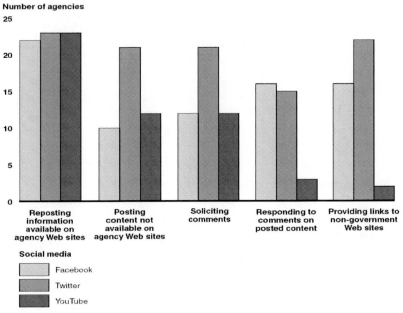

Source: GAO analysis of publicly available data.

Figure 1. Agency Use of Facebook, Twitter, and YouTube from July 2010 through January 2011.

Reposting Information Available on Agency Web sites

All 23 agencies used social media to re-post information that is also available on an official agency Web site. This information typically included press releases that agencies issue on mission-related topics or posts to an agency's blog. Each of the three services was used for reposting information by the agencies.

Facebook was used to repost information and direct the public to an agency's official Web site. For example, the Social Security Administration (SSA) posted a notice on its Facebook page that briefly discussed Social

Security benefits and provided a link to SSA's Web site. The same information was also posted on the SSA Web page.

Twitter was used to repost information in an abbreviated format, accompanied by a link to an official agency Web page where the full content was available. For example, the Department of the Interior posted a message (or "tweet") about an order that the Secretary of the Interior had issued and provided a link to the agency's Web site where the full order was available.

YouTube was generally used to provide an alternate means of accessing videos that were available on the agencies' Web sites. For example, the Department of Defense (DOD) uploaded a video to its YouTube channel—the Pentagon Channel—that described what was going on at the Pentagon during a particular week. The video was also posted on a DOD Web site dedicated to broadcasting military news and information for members of the armed forces.

Posting Content Not Available on Agency Web sites

In addition to reposting information, agencies also used social media to post original content that is not available on their Web sites. All 23 agencies used social media to post content not available on the agency's Web site. Twitter was used most often for this purpose.

Facebook was used to post content such as pictures and descriptions of officials on tours or inspections. For example, the Facebook page for the Department of Housing and Urban Development (HUD) featured a picture of the HUD Secretary with President Obama and others while visiting a renovated public housing development during a trip to New Orleans to observe efforts to rebuild the city following Hurricane Katrina. This picture and explanation were not posted to any of HUD's Web sites.

Twitter was often used by agencies to post ephemeral or time-sensitive information. For example, DOD used its Twitter account to encourage its subscribers to sign up to be extras in a movie filming in Washington, D.C. This information and encouragement were not posted on the department's Web site.

YouTube was often used to publish videos of officials discussing topics of interest to the public. An example of this is a video posted to the Department of Energy's (DOE) YouTube channel on August 2, 2010, in which an official discussed a project for a battery-based energy storage system. Neither this video nor a transcript of the video was found on a DOE Web site.

Soliciting Comments

Agencies also used Facebook, Twitter, and YouTube to request comments from the public. This feedback may be received either through the social media service itself or through an agency Web site. Twenty-two of 23 agencies used social media to solicit comments from the public. Of the 22 agencies soliciting feedback, most used Twitter for this purpose.

Facebook was generally used for feedback solicitation both when the agency wanted the public to provide comments directly via the social media site and when the agency wanted the public to provide comments through an agency Web site. For example, the Department of Veterans Affairs asked on its Facebook page if the readers liked the redesign of the agency's main Web site. The post received over 50 comments.

Twitter was generally used for feedback solicitation when the agency wanted the public to provide comments through an agency Web site. For example, the Department of Education posted a tweet that requested both teachers and parents to comment on their views of what an effective parent-teacher partnership looks like. The post included a link to the department's blog on its Web site, where individuals could leave comments.

YouTube was also used for feedback solicitation. For example, the Department of Transportation uploaded a video to its YouTube channel asking the public to create and upload videos describing how distracted driving has affected their lives. The video received multiple comments from the public expressing their views on driving and using their cell phones at the same time.

Responding to Comments on Posted Content

Agencies also used social media to respond to comments from the public that were posted on the agencies social media sites to address both administrative and mission-related topics. In these instances, agency responses to public comments were posted to the same social media Web pages where the original comments appeared. Seventeen of the 23 agencies posted responses to public comments on their social media sites. These agencies generally used Facebook or Twitter the most for this activity, with few agencies responding to comments received on their YouTube channels.

Agencies used Facebook to respond to comments received on their Facebook pages. For example, HUD posted information on its Facebook page regarding the department's allocation of funding for rental assistance for nonelderly persons with disabilities with a link to additional information located on the department's Web site. In response, individuals posted questions and comments, and HUD responded.

Twitter was also used by agencies to respond to comments.[17] For example, a tweet posted by the Small Business Administration (SBA) in response to a comment received from a Twitter user stated that the agency was still tweaking the functionality of a system and as a means to provide better customer service asked what e-mail address the individual used.

Providing Links to Non-Government Web sites

The agencies we reviewed also used social media sites to post links to non-government Web sites (i.e., a Web site whose address does not end in .gov or is not an agency initiative). For example, agencies often provided links to relevant articles located on news media Web sites. All 23 agencies used social media to post links to non-government Web sites. Of the three social media services, Twitter was used the most, while few agencies used YouTube for this purpose.

Twitter was often used by agencies to post links to Web sites, as many of the tweets that Twitter subscribers receive contain links to Web sites providing further information. For example, the Secretary of Transportation posted a Twitter message about a non-government organization's Web site, along with a link to the site.

FEDERAL AGENCIES HAVE MADE MIXED PROGRESS IN DEVELOPING POLICIES AND PROCEDURES FOR MANAGING AND PROTECTING INFORMATION ASSOCIATED WITH SOCIAL MEDIA USE

Federal agencies have made mixed progress in developing records management guidance and assessing privacy and security risks associated with their use of commercially provided social media services. Specifically, 12 of the 23 major federal agencies that use Facebook, Twitter, and YouTube have developed and issued guidance to agency officials that outlines (1) processes and policies for how social media records are identified and managed and (2) record-keeping roles and responsibilities. Further, 12 agencies have updated their privacy policies to describe whether they use personal information made available through social media. In addition, eight agencies conducted privacy impact assessments to identify potential risks associated with agency use of the three services. Finally, seven agencies assessed and documented security risks associated with use of the three services and identified mitigating controls to address those risks. Table 2 outlines the extent to which each of the 23 major federal agencies have developed policies and procedures for use of social media.

Table 2. Extent to Which Major Federal Agencies Have Developed Policies and Procedures for Using Social Media

Agency	Records management	Privacy protection		Security risk management
	Document processes and policies and record-keeping roles and responsibilities for how social media records are identified and managed	Update privacy policy to discuss use of PII made available through social media	Conduct privacy impact assessment for social media use	Identify security risks associated with agency use of social media and security controls to mitigate risks
Department of Agriculture	○	●	○	●
Department of Commerce	●	○	○	○
Department of Defense	●	●	○	●
Department of Education	○	○	◐	○
Department of Energy	●	●	●	○
Department of Health and Human Services	●	○	○	●
Department of Homeland Security	○	●	●	○
Department of Housing and Urban Development	●	●	●	○
Department of the Interior	●	●	●	●
Department of Justice	●	●	●	○
Department of Labor	●	○	●	●
Department of State	●	●	◐	○

Table 2. (Continued)

Agency	Records management — Document processes and policies and record-keeping roles and responsibilities for how social media records are identified and managed	Privacy protection — Update privacy policy to discuss use of PII made available through social media	Privacy protection — Conduct privacy impact assessment for social media use	Security risk management — Identify security risks associated with agency use of social media and security controls to mitigate risks
Department of Transportation	●	○	●	○
Department of the Treasury	○	●	○	○
Department of Veterans Affairs	○	○	○	●
Environmental Protection Agency	●	●	○	○
General Services Administration	●	○	○	●
National Aeronautics and Space Administration	○	○	○	○
National Science Foundation	○	●	●	○
Office of Personnel Management	○	●	○	○
Small Business Administration	○	○	○	○
Social Security Administration	○	○	○	○
U.S. Agency for International Development	○	○	○	○

Source: GAO analysis of agency-provided data.

● - Developed policies and procedures that guided use of Facebook, Twitter and YouTube.

◐ - Developed policies and procedures that guided use of some but not all services.

○ - Did not develop policies and procedures for use of social media services.

Agencies Have Made Progress in Establishing Guidance for Managing Social Media Records

We previously reported that agencies faced challenges in assessing whether the information they generate and receive by means of these services constitutes federal records and establishing mechanisms for capturing and preserving such records.[18] NARA's October 2010 bulletin on managing social media records highlighted, among other things, the need to ensure that social media policies and procedures articulate clear records management processes and policies and recordkeeping roles and responsibilities. Establishing such guidance can provide a basis for consistently and appropriately categorizing and preserving social media content as records.

Twelve of the 23 major federal agencies have taken steps to include records management guidance in their social media policies and procedures.[19] The scope and breadth of the guidance provided varied with each agency. Specifically, eight of the agencies included general statements directing officials responsible for social media content to conform to agency records management policies in identifying records and how to manage them. For example, the Department of Health and Human Services' social media policy stated that "records management requirements for social media technologies are similar to any other information system and shall be in conformance with existing policy" and provided a Web link to the department's records management policies. Four agencies provided more specific guidance to officials on what social media content constitutes a federal record at their respective agencies. For example, the Department of Justice issued a policy in August 2009 that included a set of questions department officials are to answer in determining the record status of content posted on agency social media pages. Officials were asked to assess, among other things, (a) whether the agency content was original and not published on other agency Web sites, (b) the duration of time the content would need to be retained, and (c) what agency entity would be responsible for preserving and monitoring the information posted on the social media site.

Officials from 10 of the 11 agencies that have not yet documented social media guidance for records management reported taking actions to develop such guidance.[20] Officials from 1 other agency (the National Science Foundation) stated that they intended to prepare guidance but did not report taking any actions to do so.

However, agency officials are still likely to need clear direction on how to assess social media records when using new technology. NARA noted in a

September 2010 study that records management staff in agencies have been overwhelmed by the speed at which agency employees are adopting new social media technologies and that social media adopters have sometimes ignored records management concerns.[21] Until agencies ensure that records management processes and policies and recordkeeping roles and responsibilities are articulated within social media policies, officials responsible for creating and administering content on agency social media sites may not be making appropriate determinations about social media records.

Agencies Continue to Face Challenges in Establishing Mechanisms for Capturing and Preserving Social Media Records

Once the need to preserve information as federal records has been established, mechanisms need to be put in place to capture such records and preserve them properly. We previously testified that establishing such mechanisms may be challenging for agencies because the types of records involved when information is collected via technologies like social media services may not be clear.[22] Officials at agencies that issued records management guidance for social media generally agreed that determining how to preserve social media content as records remains an issue. For example, officials at the Department of the Interior stated that having information with federal record value on non-government systems—such as those of commercial providers of social media—can create challenges in determining who has control over the information and how and when content should be captured for record-keeping. Participants at a roundtable discussion hosted by the National Academy of Public Administration on our behalf also confirmed capturing records as a challenge. One participant suggested that further guidance from NARA to include specific "use cases" as examples would benefit agencies in understanding what approaches can be taken to properly capture and preserve social media records.

NARA recently identified the need for further study of potential mechanisms for capturing social media content as records. In its September 2010 study, NARA noted that an agency may not have sufficient control over its content to apply records management principles due to the nature of a third-party site. Furthermore, social media technology can change quickly with functionality being added or changed that could have an impact on records management. As a result, NARA concluded that it should continue to work with other federal agencies to identify best practices for capturing and managing these records. Within its October 2010 bulletin, NARA presented a list of options for how to preserve social media records, such as Web capture tools to create local versions of sites and convert content to other formats. NARA officials stated that activities are underway to provide further assistance to agencies in determining appropriate methods for capturing social media content as federal records. Specifically, in January 2011 NARA initiated a working group in partnership with the Federal Records Council to evaluate Web 2.0 issues regarding records management and develop strategies for capturing social media content as federal records. However, NARA has yet to establish a time frame for issuing new guidance as a result of these efforts. Until guidance is developed that identifies potential mechanisms for capturing social media content as records, potentially important records of government activity may not be appropriately preserved.

Agencies Have Made Mixed Progress in Updating Privacy Policies and Assessing Privacy Risks Associated with Use of Social Media Services

Social media services often encourage people to provide extensive personal information that may be accessible to other users of those services. Government agencies that participate in such sites may have access to this information and may need to establish controls on how such information can be used. We previously reported that, while such agencies cannot control what information may be captured by social networking sites, they can make determinations about what information they will collect and how it will be used.[23] In June 2010, OMB issued memorandum M-10-23, which specified a variety of actions agencies should take to protect individual privacy whenever they use third-party Web sites and applications to engage with the public. Two key requirements established by OMB were the need for each agency to (1) update its privacy policy in order to provide the public with information on whether the agency uses PII made available through its use of third-party Web sites for any purpose, and (2) conduct privacy impact assessments (PIA) whenever an agency's use of a third-party Web site makes PII available to the agency.[24]

Assessing privacy risks is an important element of conducting a PIA because it helps agency officials determine appropriate privacy protection policies and techniques to implement those policies. A privacy risk analysis should be performed to determine the nature of privacy risks and the resulting impact if corrective actions are not implemented to mitigate those risks. Such analysis can be especially helpful in connection with the use of social media because there is a high likelihood that PII will be made available to the agency.

Twelve out of 23 agencies updated their privacy policies to include discussion on the use of personal information made available through social media services.[25] In general, agencies stated that while PII was made available to them through their use of social media services, they did not collect or use the PII. For example, HUD updated the privacy policy on its main Web site, www.hud.gov, to state that "no personally identifiable information (PII) may be requested or collected from [its use of] social media sites." As another example, the Department of Energy included a discussion of its policy of removing PII that may be posted on its social media page, noting that officials reserved the right to moderate or remove comments that include PII.

Officials from 5 of the 11 agencies that have not updated their privacy policies reported taking actions to do so.[26] Officials from 6 additional agencies (the Departments of Commerce, Health and Human Services, Labor, and Transportation; the National Aeronautics and Space Administration, and the Social Security Administration) stated that they intended to update their privacy policies but did not report taking any actions to do so.

Eight agencies conducted PIAs to assess the privacy risks associated with their use of the three services.[27] For example, the Department of Homeland Security (DHS) published a PIA that assessed the risks of the agency's use of social networking tools, including the potential for agency access to the personal information of individuals interacting with the department on such sites. To mitigate this risk, the department established a policy of prohibiting the collection of personal information by DHS officials using social media sites. Likewise, the Department of Transportation completed a PIA for the use of third-party Web sites and applications, including Facebook, Twitter, and YouTube. The PIA outlined, among other things, what types of PII may potentially be made available to the agency through its use of social media, including the name, current residence, and age of users who may friend, follow, subscribe to or otherwise interact with an official department page on a third-party site. In these instances, the department's PIA directed officials to avoid capturing and using the PII and to redact any PII contained in screenshots that may be saved for recordkeeping purposes.

Officials from 13 agencies had not completed PIAs for their use of any of the social media services, while an additional 2 agencies performed assessments that only evaluated risks associated with using Facebook. Officials from 10 of these agencies reported taking actions to conduct the assessments.[28] Officials from 2 other agencies (the Department of State and the Small Business Administration) stated that they intended to conduct assessments but did not report taking any actions to do so. Officials from the other 3 agencies (the Departments of Agriculture and the Treasury; and the General Services Administration) stated that they did not plan to conduct PIAs because they were not planning to collect personal information provided on their social media sites and, therefore, an assessment was unnecessary.

However, OMB's guidance states that when an agency takes action that causes PII to become accessible to agency officials—such as posting information on a Facebook page that allows the public to comment—PIAs are required. Given that agency officials have access to comments that may contain PII and could collect and use the information for another purpose, it is important that an assessment be conducted, even if there are no plans to save the information to an agency system.

Without updating privacy policies and performing and publishing PIAs, agency officials and the public lack assurance that all potential privacy risks have been evaluated and that protections have been identified to mitigate them.

Agencies Have Made Mixed Progress in Assessing Security Risks Associated with Use of Commercially Provided Social Media Services

Pervasive and sustained cyber attacks continue to pose a potentially devastating threat to the systems and operations of the federal government. As part of managing an effective agency-wide information security program to mitigate such threats, FISMA requires that federal agencies conduct periodic assessments of the risk and magnitude of harm that could result from the unauthorized access, use, disclosure, disruption, modification, or destruction of agency information and information systems. To help agencies implement such statutory requirements, NIST developed a risk management framework for agencies to follow in developing information security programs.[29] As part of this framework, federal agencies are to assess security risks associated with information systems that process federal agency information and identify security controls that can be used to mitigate the identified risks. In associated guidance, NIST highlighted that using such a risk-based approach is also important in circumstances where an organization is employing information technology beyond its ability to adequately protect essential missions and business functions, such as when using commercially provided social media services.[30] By identifying the potential security threats associated with use of such third-party systems, agencies can establish proper controls and restrictions on agency use.

Seven out of 23 agencies performed and documented security risk assessments concerning their use of the three social media services.[31] For example, the Department of Labor outlined the agency's use of the three tools within one risk assessment, evaluating potential threats and vulnerabilities, and recommended controls to mitigate risks associated with those threats and vulnerabilities. The department identified, among other things, the potential risk of having unauthorized information posted to its social media page by agency officials with social media responsibilities and identified the need for such individuals to receive training on proper use of social media sites. Additionally, a Department of Health and Human Services security document stated that, due to risks associated with use of social media, including the potential for social media sites to be used as a vehicle for transmitting malicious software, the department would block use of social media sites— including Facebook, Twitter, and YouTube—by employees, with specific allowances made for those with documented business needs.

According to officials, 16 agencies had not completed and documented assessments for their use of any of the social media services. Officials from 12 of these agencies reported that they were taking actions to conduct security risk assessments but had not yet completed them.[32] Officials from 2 additional agencies (the Department of Commerce and the National Science Foundation) stated that they intended to conduct assessments but did not report taking any actions to do so. Officials at 1 other agency (the Department of State) reported that they did not plan to conduct assessments because their internal policies and procedures did not require them to perform risk assessments. As we previously stated, however, NIST guidance requires the application of the risk management process to social networking uses to establish proper controls and restrictions on agency use. Officials from 1 other agency (the Department of Transportation) reported that they had conducted a security risk assessment but did not document the results. Without such documentation, the agency may lack evidence of the justification and rationale for decisions made based on the risk assessment and, consequently, the assurance that security controls have been implemented to properly address identified security threats.

Without conducting and documenting a risk assessment, agency officials cannot ensure that appropriate controls and mitigation measures are in place to address potentially heightened threats associated with social media, including spear phishing and social engineering.

CONCLUSION

Federal agencies are increasingly making use of social media technologies, including Facebook, Twitter, and YouTube, to provide information about agency activities and interact with the public. While the purposes for which agencies use these tools vary, they have the potential to improve the government's ability to disseminate information, interact with the public, and improve services to citizens.

However, the widespread use of social media technologies also introduces risks, and agencies have made mixed progress in establishing appropriate policies and procedures for managing records, protecting the privacy of personal information, and ensuring the security of federal systems and information. Specifically, just over half of the major agencies using social media have established policies and procedures for identifying what content generated by social media is necessary to preserve in order to ensure compliance with the Federal Records Act, and they continue to face challenges in effectively capturing social media content as records. Without clear policies and procedures for properly identifying and managing social media records, potentially important records of government activity may not be appropriately preserved. In addition, most agencies have not updated their privacy policies or assessed the impact their use of social media may have on the protection of personal information from improper collection, disclosure, or use, as called for in recent OMB guidance. Performing PIAs and updating privacy policies can provide individuals with better assurance that all potential privacy risks associated with their personal information have been evaluated and that protections have been identified to mitigate them. Finally, most agencies did not have documented assessments of the security risks that social media can pose to federal information or systems in alignment with FISMA requirements, which could result in the loss of sensitive information or unauthorized access to critical systems supporting the operations of the federal government. Without conducting and documenting a risk assessment, agency officials cannot ensure that appropriate controls and mitigation measures are in place to address potentially heightened threats associated with social media, such as spear phishing and social engineering.

RECOMMENDATIONS FOR EXECUTIVE ACTION

To ensure that federal agencies have adequate guidance to determine the appropriate method for preserving federal records generated by content presented on agency social media sites, we recommend that the Archivist of the United States develop guidance on effectively capturing records from social media sites and that this guidance incorporate best practices.

We are also making 32 recommendations to 21 of the 23 departments and agencies in our review to improve their development and implementation of policies and procedures for managing and protecting information associated with social media use. Appendix II contains these recommendations.

AGENCY COMMENTS AND OUR EVALUATION

We sent draft copies of this report to the 23 agencies covered by our review, as well as to the National Archives and Records Administration. We received written or e-mail responses from all the agencies. A summary of their comments and our responses, where appropriate, are provided below.

In providing written comments on a draft of this report, the Archivist of the United States stated that NARA concurred with the recommendation to develop guidance on effectively capturing records from social media sites and that the agency would incorporate best practices in this guidance. NARA's comments are reprinted in appendix III.

Of the 21 agencies to which we made recommendations, 12 (the Departments of Defense, Education, Energy, Homeland Security, Housing and Urban Development, and Veterans Affairs; the Environmental Protection Agency; the National Aeronautics and Space Administration; the National Science Foundation; the Office of Personnel Management; the Social Security Administration; and the U.S. Agency for International Development) agreed with our recommendations.

Two of the 21 agencies (the Departments of Commerce and Health and Human Services) generally agreed with our recommendations but provided qualifying comments:

- In written comments on a draft of the report, the Secretary of Commerce concurred with our two recommendations but provided qualifying comments about the second. Regarding our recommendation that the department conduct and document a security risk assessment to assess security threats associated with agency use of commercially provided social media services and identify security controls that can be used to mitigate the identified threats, he stated that the department had a policy in place that requires risk-based assessments to be conducted of social media technologies used by the department in order to determine if mitigating strategies, such as access or usage limitation, are warranted. However, the department did not provide documentation demonstrating that it had completed and documented any of the required risk assessments. The department's comments are reprinted in appendix IV.

- In an e-mail response on a draft of the report, a Department of Health and Human Services' Senior Information Security Officer stated that the department agreed with our recommendation to update its privacy policy. However, the department disagreed with the perceived finding that it had not made progress in conducting a PIA and reported recent efforts to do so. We did not intend to suggest that the department had not taken any steps to develop a PIA, and we updated our report to clarify that the department has taken actions to develop PIAs for its social media use. However, the agency has not yet completed its PIA and thus may lack assurance that all potential privacy risks have been evaluated and that protections have been identified to mitigate them.

Three of the 21 agencies (the Departments of Agriculture and State; and the General Services Administration) did not concur with all of the recommendations made to them:

- In written comments on a draft of the report, the Department of Agriculture's CIO disagreed with our recommendation that the department conduct and document a privacy impact assessment that evaluates potential privacy risks associated with agency use of social media services and identifies protections to address them. Specifically, the CIO stated that the department had completed a Privacy Threshold Analysis that indicated that a PIA was not required since the department did not solicit, collect, or retain PII through its social media sites. However, as indicated in our report, OMB's guidance states that when an agency takes action that causes PII to become accessible to agency officials—such as posting information on a Facebook page that allows the public to comment—PIAs are required. Without a PIA, the department may lack assurance that all potential privacy risks have been evaluated and that protections have been identified to mitigate them. The Department of Agriculture's comments are reprinted in appendix V.

- In written comments on a draft of the report, the Department of State's Chief Financial Officer concurred with one of our two recommendations, but not the other. Specifically, regarding our recommendation that the department conduct and document a security risk assessment to assess security threats associated with agency use of commercially provided social media services and identify security controls that can be used to mitigate the identified threats, he stated that the department shared GAO's concern regarding the security of information in commercially provided social media but that since the department had already determined that its use of social media sites would be limited to providing the public with "low-impact" information, no further risk assessment or certification and accreditation was required. He further stated that the impact on confidentiality, integrity, and availability of systems with such non-structured data could only be determined by policy, not by risk analysis and, therefore, a security risk assessment was not warranted. However, although limiting the type of information that is processed on third-party systems can be an effective mitigating security control, without conducting and documenting a risk assessment, agency officials cannot ensure that policies and mitigation measures effectively address potentially heightened threats associated with social media, including spear phishing and social engineering. The Department of State's comments are reprinted in appendix VI.

- In written comments on a draft of the report, the Administrator of the General Services Administration partially agreed with our two recommendations. Regarding our recommendation that the agency update its privacy policies to describe whether PII made available through its use of social media services is collected and used, the Administrator noted that the agency was updating its privacy directive to describe the agency's practices for handling PII made available through the use of social media. Accordingly, we have updated our report to indicate that the agency has taken actions to update its privacy policies for its use of social media. Regarding our recommendation that the agency conduct and document a privacy impact assessment that evaluates potential privacy risks associated with agency use of social media services and identifies protections to address them, the Administrator stated that no PII is sought by or provided to GSA as a result of the agency's use of Facebook, YouTube, and Twitter and, therefore, the agency determined that conducting a PIA was unnecessary. However, as indicated in our report, OMB's guidance states that when an agency takes action that causes PII to become accessible to agency officials—such as posting information on a Facebook page that allows the public to comment— PIAs are required. Without a PIA, the department may lack assurance that all potential privacy risks have been evaluated and that protections have been identified to mitigate them. The General Services Administration's comments are reprinted in appendix VII.

Four of the 21 agencies did not comment on the recommendations addressed to them. Specifically, the Departments of Labor and Transportation reported that they did not have any comments and the Department of the Treasury and Small Business Administration only provided technical comments, which we addressed in the final report as appropriate.

In cases where these 21 agencies also provided technical comments, we have addressed them in the final report as appropriate. Agencies also provided with their comments information regarding actions completed or underway to address our findings and recommendations and we updated our report to recognize those efforts.[33] Additional written comments are reprinted in appendices VIII through XVII.

We also received e-mail responses from the 2 agencies to which we did not make recommendations. Specifically, the Department of the Interior provided technical comments via e-mail and the Department of Justice stated that it did not have comments on the draft of this report.

As agreed with your office, unless you publicly announce the contents of this report earlier, we plan no further distribution until 30 days from the report date. We will then send copies of this report to other interested congressional committees, Secretaries of the Departments of Agriculture, Commerce, Defense, Education, Energy, Health and Human Services, Homeland Security, Housing and Urban Development, the Interior, Labor, State, Transportation, the Treasury, and Veterans Affairs; the Attorney General; the Administrators of the Environmental Protection Agency, General Services Administration, National Aeronautics and Space Administration, Small Business Administration, and U.S. Agency for International Development; the Commissioner of the Social Security Administration; the Directors of the National Science Foundation and Office of Personnel Management; and the

Archivist of the United States. The report will also be available at no charge on the GAO Web site at http://www.gao.gov.

If you or your staff have any questions regarding this report, please contact me at (202) 512-6244 or at wilshuseng@gao.gov. Contact points for our Offices of Congressional Relations and Public Affairs may be found on the last page of this report. Key contributors to this report are listed in appendix XVIII.

Gregory C. Wilshusen

Gregory C. Wilshusen
Director, Information Security Issues

List of Requesters

The Honorable Joseph I. Lieberman, Chairman
Committee on Homeland Security and Governmental Affairs
United States Senate

The Honorable Thomas R. Carper, Chairman
Subcommittee on Federal Financial Management, Government
Information, Federal Services, and International Security
Committee on Homeland Security and Governmental Affairs
United States Senate

The Honorable Mark L. Pryor, Chairman
Subcommittee on Disaster Recovery and Intergovernmental Affairs
Committee on Homeland Security and Governmental Affairs
United States Senate

The Honorable Elijah Cummings, Ranking Member
Committee on Oversight and Government Reform
House of Representatives
The Honorable Wm. Lacy Clay
House of Representatives

APPENDIX I. OBJECTIVES, SCOPE, AND METHODOLOGY

Our objectives were to:

- describe how agencies are currently using commercially provided social media services, and
- determine the extent to which federal agencies have developed and implemented policies and procedures for managing and protecting information associated with the use of commercially provided social media services.

To address our first objective, we examined the headquarters-level Facebook pages, Twitter accounts, and YouTube channels associated with each of the 24 major federal agencies covered by the Chief Financial Officers Act[34] to describe the types of information agencies disseminated via the services and the nature of their interactions with the public.[35] We selected these three services because of their widespread use within the federal government (23 out of 24 major agencies use each of the services) as well as their broad popularity with the public. We reviewed content on the social media pages, including agency posts as well as comments provided by the public, from July 2010 through January 2011. We categorized agency use based on types of information found on their social media pages. These categories were (1) reposting information available on agency Web sites; (2) posting content not available on agency Web sites; (3) soliciting comments; (4) responding to comments on posted content; and (5) providing links to non-government Web sites. Each agency social media page was reviewed by an analyst to determine whether information had been posted that fell into one of the five categories. Each identified example was corroborated by a second analyst. In the event no examples were identified for an agency in a specific category by the first analyst, the second analyst conducted an additional independent review of agency posts to confirm that none existed.

To address our second objective, we reviewed pertinent records management, privacy, and security policies, procedures, guidance, and risk assessments in place at each of the 23 federal agencies and compared them to relevant federal records management, privacy, and security laws, regulations, and guidance.[36] These included the Federal Records Act, the Privacy Act of 1974, the E-Government Act of 2002, the Federal Information Security Management Act of 2002 (FISMA), as well as guidance from the National Archives and Records Administration (NARA), Office of Management and

Budget (OMB), and National Institute of Standards and Technology (NIST). We interviewed officials at each of these agencies to discuss recent efforts to oversee the development of social media policies and procedures and assess risks. We also reviewed relevant reports and studies to identify records management, privacy, and security risks associated with social media use by federal agencies. We interviewed officials from OMB, NARA, and NIST, and members of the Chief Information Officer Council to develop further understanding of federal agency requirements for properly managing and protecting information associated with social media use. Further, we coordinated with the National Academy of Public Administration, which hosted a roundtable discussion on our behalf where views on these issues were solicited from federal agency officials involved in agency use of social media. Finally, we interviewed representatives of Facebook, Twitter, and YouTube to discuss records management, privacy, and security issues and their current and planned approaches regarding interactions with federal agencies.

We conducted this performance audit from July 2010 to June 2011 in the Washington, D.C., area, in accordance with generally accepted government auditing standards. Those standards require that we plan and perform the audit to obtain sufficient, appropriate evidence to provide a reasonable basis for our findings and conclusions based on our audit objectives. We believe that the evidence obtained provides a reasonable basis for our findings and conclusions based on our audit objectives.

APPENDIX II.
RECOMMENDATIONS TO DEPARTMENTS AND AGENCIES

Department of Agriculture

To ensure that appropriate privacy measures are in place when commercially provided social media services are used, we recommend that the Secretary of Agriculture take the following action:

- Conduct and document a privacy impact assessment that evaluates potential privacy risks associated with agency use of social media services and identifies protections to address them.

Department of Commerce

To ensure that appropriate privacy and security measures are in place when commercially provided social media services are used, we recommend that the Secretary of Commerce take the following two actions:

- Update privacy policies to describe whether PII made available through use of social media services is collected and used.

- Conduct and document a security risk assessment to assess security threats associated with agency use of commercially provided social media services and identify security controls that can be used to mitigate the identified threats.

Department of Defense

To ensure that appropriate privacy and security measures are in place when commercially provided social media services are used, we recommend that the Secretary of Defense take the following action:

- Conduct and document a privacy impact assessment that evaluates potential privacy risks associated with agency use of social media services and identifies protections to address them.

Department of Education

To ensure that appropriate privacy measures are in place when commercially provided social media services are used, we recommend that the Secretary of Education take the following action:

- Update privacy policies to describe whether PII made available through use of social media services is collected and used.

Department of Energy

To ensure that appropriate security measures are in place when commercially provided social media services are used, we recommend that the Secretary of Energy take the following action:

- Conduct and document a security risk assessment to assess security threats associated with agency use of commercially provided social media services and identify security controls that can be used to mitigate the identified threats.

Department of Health and Human Services

To ensure that appropriate privacy measures are in place when commercially provided social media services are used, we recommend that the Secretary of Health and Human Services take the following action:

- Update privacy policies to describe whether PII made available through use of social media services is collected and used.

Department of Homeland Security

To ensure that appropriate security measures are in place when commercially provided social media services are used, we recommend that the Secretary of Homeland Security take the following action:

- Conduct and document a security risk assessment to assess security threats associated with agency use of commercially provided social media services and identify security controls that can be used to mitigate the identified threats.

Department of Housing and Urban Development

To ensure that appropriate security measures are in place when commercially provided social media services are used, we recommend that the Secretary of Housing and Urban Development take the following action:

- Conduct and document a security risk assessment to assess security threats associated with agency use of Twitter and YouTube and identify security controls that can be used to mitigate the identified threats.

Department of Labor

To ensure that appropriate privacy measures are in place when commercially provided social media services are used, we recommend that the Secretary of Labor take the following action:

- Update privacy policies to describe whether PII made available through use of social media services is collected and used.

Department of State

To ensure that appropriate privacy and security measures are in place when commercially provided social media services are used, we recommend that the Secretary of State take the following two actions:

- Conduct and document a privacy impact assessment that evaluates potential privacy risks associated with agency use of Twitter and YouTube and identifies protections to address them.

- Conduct and document a security risk assessment to assess security threats associated with agency use of commercially provided social media services and identify security controls that can be used to mitigate the identified threats.

Department of Transportation

To ensure that appropriate privacy and security measures are in place when commercially provided social media services are used, we recommend that the Secretary of Transportation take the following two actions:

- Update privacy policies to describe whether PII made available through use of social media services is collected and used.

- Conduct and document a security risk assessment to assess security threats associated with agency use of commercially provided social media services and identify security controls that can be used to mitigate the identified threats.

Department of the Treasury

To ensure that appropriate privacy measures are in place when commercially provided social media services are used, we recommend that the Secretary of the Treasury take the following action:

- Conduct and document a privacy impact assessment that evaluates potential privacy risks associated with agency use of social media services and identifies protections to address them.

Department of Veterans Affairs

To ensure that appropriate records management and privacy measures are in place when commercially provided social media services are used, we recommend that the Secretary of Veterans Affairs take the following two actions:

- Add records management guidance to agency social media policies that describes records management processes and policies and recordkeeping roles and responsibilities.

- Conduct and document a privacy impact assessment that evaluates potential privacy risks associated with agency use of social media services and identifies protections to address them.

Environmental Protection Agency

To ensure that appropriate privacy and security measures are in place when commercially provided social media services are used, we recommend that the Administrator of the Environmental Protection Agency take the following two actions:

- Conduct and document a privacy impact assessment that evaluates potential privacy risks associated with agency use of social media services and identifies protections to address them.

- Conduct and document a security risk assessment to assess security threats associated with agency use of commercially provided social media services and identify security controls that can be used to mitigate the identified threats.

General Services Administration

To ensure that appropriate privacy measures are in place when commercially provided social media services are used, we recommend that the Administrator of the General Services Administration take the following two actions:

- Update privacy policies to describe whether PII made available through use of social media services is collected and used.

- Conduct and document a privacy impact assessment that evaluates potential privacy risks associated with agency use of social media services and identifies protections to address them.

National Aeronautics and Space Administration

To ensure that appropriate privacy and security measures are in place when commercially provided social media services are used, we recommend that the Administrator of the National Aeronautics and Space Administration take the following three actions:

- Update privacy policies to describe whether PII made available through use of social media services is collected and used.

- Conduct and document a privacy impact assessment that evaluates potential privacy risks associated with agency use of social media services and identifies protections to address them.

- Conduct and document a security risk assessment to assess security threats associated with agency use of commercially provided social media services and identify security controls that can be used to mitigate the identified threats.

National Science Foundation

To ensure that appropriate records management and security measures are in place when commercially provided social media services are used, we recommend that the Director of the National Science Foundation take the following two actions:

- Add records management guidance to agency social media policies that describes records management processes and policies and recordkeeping roles and responsibilities.

- Conduct and document a security risk assessment to assess security threats associated with agency use of commercially provided social media services and identify security controls that can be used to mitigate the identified threats.

Office of Personnel Management

To ensure that appropriate privacy and security measures are in place when commercially provided social media services are used, we recommend that the Director of the Office of Personnel Management take the following two actions:

- Conduct and document a privacy impact assessment that evaluates potential privacy risks associated with agency use of social media services and identifies protections to address them.

- Conduct and document a security risk assessment to assess security threats associated with agency use of commercially provided social media services and identify security controls that can be used to mitigate the identified threats.

Small Business Administration

To ensure that appropriate privacy measures are in place when commercially provided social media services are used, we recommend that the Administrator of the Small Business Administration take the following action:

- Conduct and document a privacy impact assessment that evaluates potential privacy risks associated with agency use of social media services and identifies protections to address them.

Social Security Administration

To ensure that appropriate privacy measures are in place when commercially provided social media services are used, we recommend that the Commissioner of the Social Security Administration take the following action:

- Update privacy policies to describe whether PII made available through use of social media services is collected and used.

U.S. Agency for International Development

To ensure that appropriate records management and security measures are in place when commercially provided social media services are used, we recommend that the Administrator of the U.S. Agency for International Development take the following two actions:

- Add records management guidance to agency social media policies that describes records management processes and policies and recordkeeping roles and responsibilities.
- Conduct and document a security risk assessment to assess security threats associated with agency use of commercially provided social

media services and identify security controls that can be used to mitigate the identified threats.

Appendix III.
Comments from the National Archives and Records Administration

NATIONAL ARCHIVES

Via email

MAY 2 4 2011

Gregory C. Wilshusen
Director, Information Security Issues
United States Government Accountability Office
44 G Street, NW
Washington, DC 20548

Dear Mr. Wilshusen,

Thank you for the opportunity to review and comment on the draft report GAO-11-605, *SOCIAL MEDIA: Federal Agencies Need Policies and Procedures for Managing and Protecting Information They Access and Disseminate.* We are pleased to note the positive recognition of our October 2010 bulletin on managing social media records as a basis for consistently and appropriately categorizing and preserving social media content as records.

We concur with the recommendation that NARA develop guidance on effectively capturing records from social media sites, and will incorporate best practices in this guidance.

If you have questions regarding this information, please contact Mary Drak by email at mary.drak@nara.gov or by phone at 301-837-1668.

David S. Ferriero
Archivist of the United States

APPENDIX IV.
COMMENTS FROM THE DEPARTMENT OF COMMERCE

Note: GAO's comments supplementing those in the report's text appear at the end of this appendix. See comment 1.

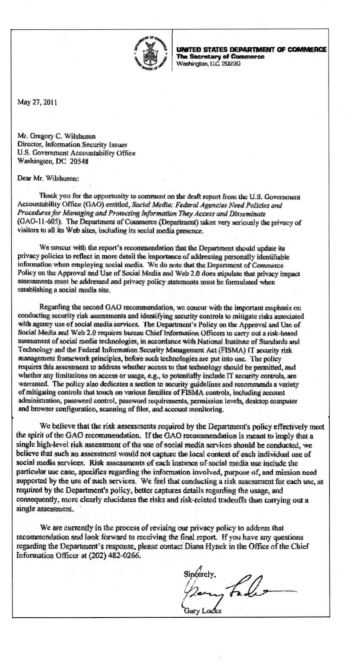

UNITED STATES DEPARTMENT OF COMMERCE
The Secretary of Commerce
Washington, D.C. 20230

May 27, 2011

Mr. Gregory C. Wilshusen
Director, Information Security Issues
U.S. Government Accountability Office
Washington, DC 20548

Dear Mr. Wilshusen:

Thank you for the opportunity to comment on the draft report from the U.S. Government Accountability Office (GAO) entitled, *Social Media: Federal Agencies Need Policies and Procedures for Managing and Protecting Information They Access and Disseminate* (GAO-11-605). The Department of Commerce (Department) takes very seriously the privacy of visitors to all its Web sites, including its social media presence.

We concur with the report's recommendation that the Department should update its privacy policies to reflect in more detail the importance of addressing personally identifiable information when employing social media. We do note that the Department of Commerce Policy on the Approval and Use of Social Media and Web 2.0 does stipulate that privacy impact assessments must be addressed and privacy policy statements must be formulated when establishing a social media site.

Regarding the second GAO recommendation, we concur with the important emphasis on conducting security risk assessments and identifying security controls to mitigate risks associated with agency use of social media services. The Department's Policy on the Approval and Use of Social Media and Web 2.0 requires bureau Chief Information Officers to carry out a risk-based assessment of social media technologies, in accordance with National Institute of Standards and Technology and the Federal Information Security Management Act (FISMA) IT security risk management framework principles, before such technologies are put into use. The policy requires this assessment to address whether access to that technology should be permitted, and whether any limitations on access or usage, e.g., to potentially include IT security controls, are warranted. The policy also dedicates a section to security guidelines and recommends a variety of mitigating controls that touch on various families of FISMA controls, including account administration, password control, password requirements, permission levels, desktop computer and browser configuration, scanning of files, and account monitoring.

We believe that the risk assessments required by the Department's policy effectively meet the spirit of the GAO recommendation. If the GAO recommendation is meant to imply that a single high-level risk assessment of the use of social media services should be conducted, we believe that such an assessment would not capture the local context of each individual use of social media services. Risk assessments of each instance of social media use include the particular use case, specifics regarding the information involved, purpose of, and mission need supported by the use of such services. We feel that conducting a risk assessment for each use, as required by the Department's policy, better captures details regarding the usage, and consequently, more clearly elucidates the risks and risk-related tradeoffs than carrying out a single assessment.

We are currently in the process of revising our privacy policy to address that recommendation and look forward to receiving the final report. If you have any questions regarding the Department's response, please contact Diana Hynek in the Office of the Chief Information Officer at (202) 482-0266.

Sincerely,

Gary Locke

The following are GAO's comments to the U.S. Department of Commerce's letter dated May 27, 2011.

GAO Comments

1. The department did not provide documentation demonstrating that it had completed and documented any of the required risk assessments.

APPENDIX V. COMMENTS FROM THE U.S. DEPARTMENT OF AGRICULTURE

Note: GAO's comments supplementing those in the report's text appear at the end of this appendix.

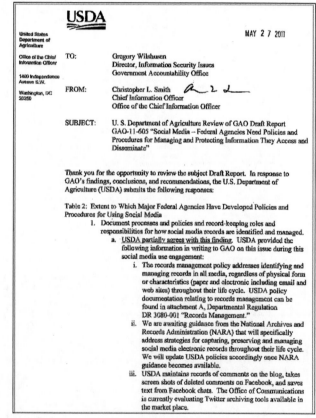

See comment 1. See comment 2. See comment 3.

iv. USDA is currently in the process of drafting a social media record keeping System of Records Notice.

Since the completion of GAO's engagement at USDA, the Department has completed its draft policy titled "New Media Roles, Responsibilities and Authorities" (attachment B). This draft policy addresses records management across all aspects of Web 2.0 media. This draft policy is currently under internal USDA review.

2. Update Privacy policy to discuss use of Personally Identifiable Information (PII) made available through social media.
    a. USDA partially agrees with this finding. USDA has updated their Privacy Policy Statement on its social media web site to specifically address Privacy Act protected data. Please see screen shot from USDA's Social Media and Tools web page (attachment C).
    b. Additionally, USDA has updated its Privacy Policy, draft Departmental Regulation 3515-XXX (attachment D) to address the collection of PII via USDA web sites:
        "Every USDA Web site must clearly and concisely inform visitors about what information the Web site collects about individuals, why the information is collected, and how it is used. No agency/mission area will collect personal information about individuals when they visit USDA Web sites unless the visitor chooses to provide that information"

3. Conduct Privacy Impact Assessment (PIA) for social media use.
    a. USDA disagrees with this finding. USDA completed a Privacy Threshold Analysis (PTA) on the use of social media by USDA on September 14, 2010 (attachment E). The results of this PTA indicate that a PIA is not required for social media use within USDA.

GAO recommendation to USDA:

Conduct and document a PIA that evaluates potential privacy risks associated with agency use of social media services and identifies protections to address them.

USDA Response:

USDA completed a PTA on the use of social media as a public communications vehicle on September 14, 2010. The results of the PTA indicated that a PIA was not required as USDA does not solicit, collect or retain PII through its social media sites.

USDA uses social media to increase its public information outreach programs beyond USDA.gov internet web presence. USDA does not solicit nor collect PII from the public via its social media presence. Please see the attachment E,

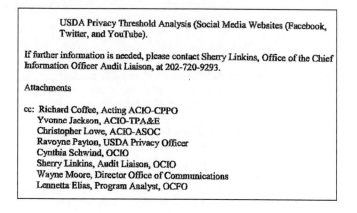

USDA Privacy Threshold Analysis (Social Media Websites (Facebook, Twitter, and YouTube).

If further information is needed, please contact Sherry Linkins, Office of the Chief Information Officer Audit Liaison, at 202-720-9293.

Attachments

cc: Richard Coffee, Acting ACIO-CPPO
     Yvonne Jackson, ACIO-TPA&E
     Christopher Lowe, ACIO-ASOC
     Ravoyne Payton, USDA Privacy Officer
     Cynthia Schwind, OCIO
     Sherry Linkins, Audit Liaison, OCIO
     Wayne Moore, Director Office of Communications
     Lennetta Elias, Program Analyst, OCFO

The following are GAO's comments to the U.S. Department of Agriculture's letter dated May 27, 2011.

GAO Comments

1. After reviewing additional documentation and comments provided by department representatives, we updated our report to indicate that the department asserted that it is taking actions to develop records management guidance for social media use, although it has not yet been completed. We have not evaluated these actions.

2. After reviewing the updated privacy policy on the Department's Web site, we agree that the agency has met the requirement, and we have modified table 2 in the final report to reflect that the department has updated its policy.

3. We believe that a PIA is required. As indicated in our report, OMB's guidance states that when an agency takes action that causes PII to become accessible to agency officials—such as posting information on a Facebook page that allows the public to comment—PIAs are required. Without a PIA, the department may lack assurance that all potential privacy risks have been evaluated and that protections have been identified to mitigate them.

APPENDIX VI.
COMMENTS FROM THE DEPARTMENT OF STATE

Note: GAO's comments supplementing those in the report's text appear at the end of this appendix.

United States Department of State

Chief Financial Officer

Washington, D.C. 20520

Ms. Jacquelyn Williams-Bridgers
Managing Director
International Affairs and Trade
Government Accountability Office
441 G Street, N.W.   MAY 3 1 2011
Washington, D.C. 20548-0001

Dear Ms. Williams-Bridgers:

 We appreciate the opportunity to review your draft report, "SOCIAL MEDIA: Federal Agencies Need Policies and Procedures for Managing and Protecting Information They Access and Disseminate," GAO Job Code 311048.

 The enclosed Department of State comments are provided for incorporation with this letter as an appendix to the final report.

 If you have any questions concerning this response, please contact Christina Jones, Privacy Division Chief, Bureau of Administration at (202) 261-8407 and George Moore, Chief Computer Scientist, Bureau of Information Resource Management at (703) 812-2203.

      Sincerely,

      James L. Millette

cc: GAO – Greg Wilshusen
  A – William H. Moser
  IRM – Susan H. Swart
  State/OIG – Evelyn Klemstine

See comment 1.
See comment 2.

Department of State Comments on GAO Draft Report

<u>SOCIAL MEDIA: Federal Agencies Need Policies and Procedures for Managing and Protecting Information They Access and Disseminate</u>
(GAO-11-605O GAO Code 311048)

The Department of State appreciates the opportunity to comment on GAO's draft report, *"SOCIAL MEDIA: Federal Agencies Need Policies and Procedures for Managing and Protecting Information They Access and Disseminate."*

Recommendation: Conduct and document a privacy impact assessment that evaluates potential privacy risks associated with agency use of Twitter and YouTube and identifies protections to address them.

Response: The Department concurs with the recommendation and has reviewed its current policy on privacy impact assessments (PIA). To that end, the Department will revise the current Facebook PIA to reflect a more comprehensive risk assessment that will incorporate all social media technologies, such as YouTube and Twitter.

Recommendation: Conduct and document a security risk assessment to assess security threats associated with agency use of commercially provided social media services and identify security controls that can be used to mitigate the identified threats.

Response: The Department shares GAO's concern regarding the security of information in commercially provided social media. However, the Department disagrees with the GAO recommendation, as stated.

The State Internet Steering Committee recently developed a policy for State officials who use such sites in an official capacity. This policy is being incorporated into training modules and user agreements to ensure that these officials keep sensitive information off of these sites. The Department has already determined that use of social media sites to provide communication with the public is a valuable tool so long as only low-impact information is provided. Moreover, as long as this policy is followed, no further risk assessment and/or certification and accreditation is required.

Note that no a-priori risk assessment of these sites is likely to provide meaningful results, since the data is non-structured, and uninformed users could (if careless or malicious) place sensitive information on these sites, just as they could currently leak it to the press. The impact on confidentiality, integrity, and availability of systems with such non-structured data can only be determined by policy (limit data to low-impact data, for example), not by risk analysis. Therefore, in our view a Security Risk Assessment at State is not warranted at this time.

The following are GAO's comments to the Department of State's letter dated May 31, 2011.

GAO Comments

1. After reviewing additional comments provided by department representatives, we updated our report to indicate that the department has plans to develop a PIA for its use of YouTube and Twitter.

2. We believe that conducting and documenting a risk assessment is necessary. Although limiting the type of information that is processed on third-party systems can be an effective mitigating security control, without conducting and documenting a risk assessment, agency officials cannot ensure that appropriate controls and mitigation measures are in place to address potentially heightened threats associated with social media, including spear phishing and social engineering.

APPENDIX VII. COMMENTS FROM THE GENERAL SERVICES ADMINISTRATION

Note: GAO's comments supplementing those in the report's text appear at the end of this appendix. See comment 1.

June 3, 2011

The Administrator

The Honorable Gene L. Dodaro
Comptroller General of the United States
U.S. Government Accountability Office
Washington, DC 20548

Dear Mr. Dodaro:

The U.S. General Services Administration (GSA) appreciates the opportunity to review and comment on the draft report, "Social Media: Federal Agencies Need Policies and Procedures for Managing and Protecting Information They Access and Disseminate" (GAO-11-605). The U.S. Government Accountability Office (GAO) recommends that the GSA Administrator ensure that appropriate privacy measures are in place when commercially provided social media services are used. GAO recommended two specific actions for GSA, discussed below. We agree in part to both recommendations. GSA is in the process of updating our privacy policy and provides clarifying information regarding GSA's use of Privacy Impact Assessments (PIA's).

<u>Recommendation 1</u>: GAO recommends GSA "[u]pdate privacy policies to describe whether PII made available through use of social media services is collected and used."

GSA takes its responsibilities regarding the protection of individuals' PII seriously. For example, GSA's new Social Media Navigator, available at www.gsa.gov/socialmedia, states the Agency's privacy policy relative to social media. It contains:

> **Privacy Considerations:** The Government requires public-facing websites to conduct privacy impact assessments if they collect personally identifiable information. They should post a "Privacy Act Statement" that describes the Agency's legal authority for collecting personal data and how the data will be used. Privacy policies on each website are also required in a standardized machine-readable format such as the Platform for Privacy Preferences Project, or P3P. Information on Web 2.0 platforms is accessible by others, so do not disclose Privacy Act protected information or other personally identifiable information unless authorized to do so in that medium.

Furthermore, since our initial meetings with GAO, the Privacy Office studied other agencies' privacy policies that incorporate guidance relative to social media. Accordingly, GSA is updating its Privacy Directive to state the Agency's practice of handling PII when it is made available through the use of social media. The revised directive will be posted when it has completed the concurrence process.

<u>Recommendation 2</u>: GAO recommends GSA "[c]onduct and document a privacy impact assessment that evaluates potential privacy risks associated with agency use of social media services and identifies protections to address them."

U.S. General Services Administration
1275 First Street, NE
Washington, DC 20417
Telephone: (202) 501-0800
Fax: (202) 219-1243

See comment 2.

GAO limited its review to Facebook, Twitter, and YouTube. As discussed on an April 14 teleconference and through additional information provided Mr. Marinos relative to the draft statement of facts, we would like to clarify here again that GSA uses Facebook, YouTube, and Twitter for one-way marketing. No PII is sought or provided to GSA as a result of our use of Facebook, YouTube, or Twitter. Therefore, a PIA is unnecessary. In contrast, when GSA plans to use social media providers for two-way communication wherein PII is potentially received from the public, GSA does indeed "conduct and document a privacy impact assessment that evaluates potential privacy risks associated with agency use of social media services and identifies protections to address them." Furthermore, GSA publically posts its PIAs as illustrated by these examples:

Challenge Post PIA
http://www.gsa.gov/graphics/staffoffices/ChallengeGovPIA.doc

Citizen Engagement PIA
http://www.gsa.gov/graphics/staffoffices/CEP_Tools_PIA_061810.doc

Open Government Citizen Engagement Tool
http://www.gsa.gov/graphics/staffoffices/OpenGovEngagementToolOCSC_021610.doc

Technical comments that update and clarify statements in the draft report are enclosed. Should you have any questions, please do not hesitate to contact me. Staff inquiries may be directed to Ms. Casey Coleman, Chief Information Officer. She can be reached at (202) 501-1000.

Sincerely,

Martha Johnson
Administrator

Enclosure

cc: Mr. Gregory C. Wilshusen,
    Director, Information Technology Security Issues
    GAO

The following are GAO's comments to the General Services Administration's letter dated June 3, 2011.

GAO Comments

1. After reviewing additional comments provided by agency representatives, we updated our report to indicate that the agency asserted that it is taking actions to develop privacy policies addressing the agency's use of PII made available through social media services. We have not evaluated these actions.

2. We believe that a PIA is required. As indicated in our report, OMB's guidance states that when an agency takes action that causes PII to become accessible to agency officials—such as posting information on a Facebook page that allows the public to comment—PIAs are required. Without a PIA, the agency may lack assurance that all potential privacy risks have been evaluated and that protections have been identified to mitigate them

APPENDIX VIII.
COMMENTS FROM THE DEPARTMENT OF DEFENSE

Note: GAO's comments supplementing those in the report's text appear at the beginning of this appendix.

The following are GAO's comments to the Department of Defense's letter dated May 27, 2011.

GAO Comments

1. We updated our report to indicate that the department asserted that it is taking actions to develop a PIA for its social media use, although it has not yet been finalized. We have not evaluated these actions.

2. After reviewing the additional documentation provided, we agree that the department met the requirement of conducting and documenting a security risk assessment. We modified the report, as appropriate, and removed the recommendation.

ASSISTANT SECRETARY OF DEFENSE
6000 DEFENSE PENTAGON
WASHINGTON, D.C. 20301-6000

MAY 2 7 2011

NETWORKS AND INFORMATION
INTEGRATION

Mr. Gregory C. Wilshusen
Director, Information Security Issues
U.S. Government Accountability Office
441 G Street, NW
Washington, DC 20548

Dear Mr. Wilshusen:

In response to the GAO Draft Report, GAO-11-605, "SOCIAL MEDIA: Federal Agencies Need Policies and Procedures for Managing and Protecting Information They Access and Disseminate," dated May 6, 2011 (GAO Code 311048), the Department of Defense concurs with the first of the two recommendations. A privacy impact assessment that evaluates potential privacy risks associated with agency use of social media services and identifies protections to address those risks has been conducted. Documentation is in the final approval process and is planned for completion by July 29, 2011.

Regarding the second recommendation, documentation of the assessment of security risks associated with DoD use of social media and identification of security controls that can be used to mitigate the identified risks was provided to your office on May 12, 2011. Consequently, your office has agreed to omit this recommendation from the final report.

The point of contact for this matter is Mr. Terry Davis, at email: terry.w.davis@osd.mil and telephone: 703-699-0107.

Sincerely,

Teresa M. Takai
Principal Deputy

See comment 1. See comment 2.

APPENDIX IX.
COMMENTS FROM THE DEPARTMENT OF EDUCATION

Note: GAO's comments supplementing those in the report's text appear at the end of this appendix.

See comment 1.

UNITED STATES DEPARTMENT OF EDUCATION

OFFICE OF COMMUNICATIONS AND OUTREACH

THE ASSISTANT SECRETARY

Mr. Gregory C. Wilshusen
Director, Information Security Issues
U.S. Government Accountability Office
441 G Street, NW
Washington, DC 20548

Dear Mr. Wilshusen:

I am writing in response to the recommendation made in the U.S. Government
Accountability Office (GAO) draft report, "Social Media: Federal Agencies Need
Policies and Procedures for Managing and Protecting Information They Access and
Disseminate" (GAO-11-605). I appreciate the opportunity to comment on the draft report
on behalf of the U.S. Department of Education (Department).

Social media tools are important to the Department's efforts to communicate with the
public. We are using Facebook, Twitter, You Tube, and a blog to share information and
engage the public in a conversation about improving education. (See our list of social
media pages and accounts at http://www2.ed.gov/about/overview/focus/social-
media.html.) And we are taking steps to ensure that when we use social media, we meet
our legal obligations and requirements.

The Department's response to the report's recommendation follows, along with
additional comments on Table 2 in the report.

Recommendation: *To ensure that appropriate privacy measures are in place when
commercially provided social media services are used, we recommend that the Secretary
of Education take the following action.*
- *Update privacy policies to describe whether PII made available through use of
social media services is collected and used.*

Response: The Department agrees with GAO's recommendation. Our privacy policy
has been updated to describe how we treat personally identifiable information (PII). The
policy includes the following statement:

"...please be aware that the privacy protection provided at ED.gov may not be available
on [these] third-party sites. Please note that when ED uses social media sites, ED does
not collect or in any way use personally identifiable information."

To read our complete privacy policy, please see the materials at the following Web
address: http://www2.ed.gov/notices/privacy/index.html#social-media.

See comment 2.

See comment 3.

See comment 4.

In addition, the Department would like to comment on several points in the draft report.

1. Table 2 in the draft report indicates that the Department has not "document[ed] processes and policies and record-keeping roles and responsibilities for how social media records are identified and managed."

The Privacy, Information, and Records Management Services team in our Office of Management developed and distributed for comment in early May 2011 draft guidance for records management related to social media. This guidance describes the principles and questions that the Department's principal offices and staff will use when analyzing, scheduling, and managing records related to social media. This guidance is under review within the Department, and we expect it to be issued in final form by the end of fiscal year (FY) 2011.

2. Table 2 indicates that the Department has not "conduct[ed] privacy impact assessment for social media use."

The Privacy, Information, and Records Management Services team in the Department's Office of Management developed and distributed in early May 2011 a draft "Privacy Impact Assessment for Social Media Websites and Applications." This draft is under review within the Department, and we expect it to be issued in final form by the end of FY 2011.

This draft privacy impact assessment (PIA) covers all Department current and authorized social media Web sites and applications that are functionally comparable, including those owned by the Department or by a third party. None of the social media Web sites and applications covered by the PIA solicit, collect, maintain, or disseminate sensitive PII from individuals who interact with these authorized social media Web sites and applications. For any social media uses that raise privacy risks that are distinct and different from those covered by this PIA, the Department will prepare a separate PIA.

3. Table 2 indicates that the Department has not "identify[ed] security risks associated with agency use of social media and security controls to mitigate risks."

We have in fact taken steps to identify and contain security risks by significantly limiting social media access and use to only those Department staff who have articulated a business need for such access or use. We have also conducted a security risk assessment of social media. This risk assessment recommends policy, procedural, and technical mitigations that may be employed to lessen the potential impact of these risks. The risk assessment is in draft and has not yet been finalized.

4. Finally, we have developed a draft comprehensive social media policy for the Department that will govern the use of social media for all employees. This policy discusses privacy, security, records management, and related legal requirements. The

development of its contents was coordinated with the development of the above-mentioned records management policy and PIA. This social media policy is currently under review within the Department, and we expect it to be issued in final form by the end of FY 2011.

We appreciate the opportunity to review the draft report and comment on the recommendation. If you have any questions or concerns regarding our response, please have your staff contact Kirk Winters at (202) 401-3540 or kirk.winters@ed.gov.

Sincerely,   5/25/11

Peter Cunningham
Assistant Secretary

The following are GAO's comments to the Department of Education's letter dated May 25, 2011.

GAO Comments

1. After reviewing the privacy policy on the department's Web site, we updated our report to indicate that the department asserted that it is taking actions to develop privacy policies addressing the agency's use of PII made available through social media services. We confirmed these actions.

2. After reviewing additional efforts stated by the department, we updated our report to indicate that the department asserted that it is taking actions to develop records management guidance for social media use, although such guidance has not yet been finalized. We have not evaluated these actions.

3. After reviewing additional efforts stated by the department, we updated our report to indicate that the department asserted that it is taking actions to conduct and document a PIA related to its use of social media, although it has not yet been finalized. We have not evaluated these actions.

4. After reviewing additional efforts stated by the department, we updated our report to indicate that the department asserted that it is taking actions to conduct and document a security risk assessment related to its use of social media, although the assessment has not yet been finalized. We have not evaluated these actions.

APPENDIX X. COMMENTS FROM THE DEPARTMENT OF HOMELAND SECURITY

Note: GAO's comments supplementing those in the report's text appear at the end of this appendix.

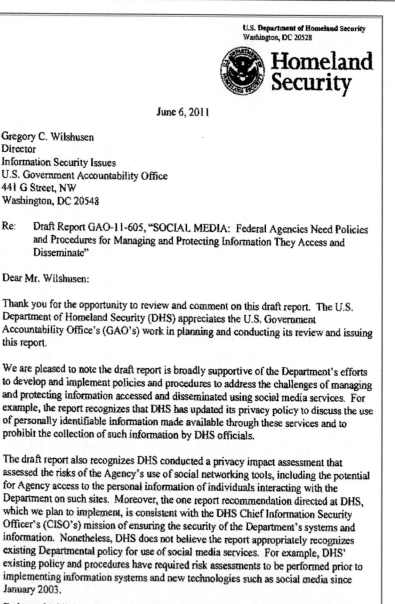

U.S. Department of Homeland Security
Washington, DC 20528

Homeland Security

June 6, 2011

Gregory C. Wilshusen
Director
Information Security Issues
U.S. Government Accountability Office
441 G Street, NW
Washington, DC 20548

Re: Draft Report GAO-11-605, "SOCIAL MEDIA: Federal Agencies Need Policies and Procedures for Managing and Protecting Information They Access and Disseminate"

Dear Mr. Wilshusen:

Thank you for the opportunity to review and comment on this draft report. The U.S. Department of Homeland Security (DHS) appreciates the U.S. Government Accountability Office's (GAO's) work in planning and conducting its review and issuing this report.

We are pleased to note the draft report is broadly supportive of the Department's efforts to develop and implement policies and procedures to address the challenges of managing and protecting information accessed and disseminated using social media services. For example, the report recognizes that DHS has updated its privacy policy to discuss the use of personally identifiable information made available through these services and to prohibit the collection of such information by DHS officials.

The draft report also recognizes DHS conducted a privacy impact assessment that assessed the risks of the Agency's use of social networking tools, including the potential for Agency access to the personal information of individuals interacting with the Department on such sites. Moreover, the one report recommendation directed at DHS, which we plan to implement, is consistent with the DHS Chief Information Security Officer's (CISO's) mission of ensuring the security of the Department's systems and information. Nonetheless, DHS does not believe the report appropriately recognizes existing Departmental policy for use of social media services. For example, DHS' existing policy and procedures have required risk assessments to be performed prior to implementing information systems and new technologies such as social media since January 2003.

To better highlight policy requirements related to the new social media technologies, in July 2009, DHS established a separate section in the policy dedicated to social media (Section 3.16 – Social Media, *DHS Sensitive Systems Policy Directive 4300A*).

See comment 1.

In late May 2011, DHS also finalized the *DHS 4300A Sensitive Systems Handbook, Attachment X – Social Media.* Attachment X expands on the existing DHS policy provided in Section 3.16 - *Social Media, DHS Sensitive Systems Policy Directive 4300A,* and DHS Management Directive (MD) 4400.1, *Web (Internet, Intranet, and Extranet Information) and Information Systems.*

Attachment X also provides information security guidance regarding official (work-related) and unofficial (personal) social media use within and outside the Department network. It specifically describes the governance of social media sites across DHS and addresses the use of social media technologies in three scenarios:

- Required Work-Related Use
- Unofficial/Personal Use at Work
- Unofficial/Personal Use Outside of Work

Additionally, Attachment X addresses social media and its associated risks and best practices and guidance regarding social media use by DHS employees and contractors.

The draft report contained one recommendation directed to DHS. Specifically, to ensure that appropriate security measures are in place when commercially-provided social media services are used, GAO recommend that the Secretary of Homeland Security:

Recommendation: Conduct and document a security risk assessment to assess security threats associated with agency use of commercially-provided social media services and identify security controls that can be used to mitigate the identified threats.

Response: Concur. The DHS CISO will conduct and document the recommended security risk assessment. Estimated completion date: March 1, 2012.

Again, thank you for the opportunity to review and comment on this draft report. We look forward to working with you on future Homeland Security issues.

Sincerely,

Jim H. Crumpacker
Director
Departmental GAO/OIG Liaison Office

The following are GAO's comments to the Department of Homeland Security's letter dated June 6, 2011.

GAO Comments

1. After reviewing additional efforts stated by the department, we updated our report to indicate that the department asserted that it is taking actions to conduct and document a security risk assessment related to its use of social media, although the assessment has not yet been finalized. We have not evaluated these actions.

Appendix XI. Comments from the Department of Housing and Urban Development

Note: GAO's comments supplementing those in the report's text appear at the end of this appendix.

See comment 1.

U.S. DEPARTMENT OF HOUSING AND URBAN DEVELOPMENT
WASHINGTON, DC 20410-3000

CHIEF INFORMATION OFFICER

MAY 2 7 2011

Mr. Gregory C. Wilshusen
Director,
Information Technology
U.S. Government Accountability Office
441 G Street, NW
Washington, DC 20548

Dear Mr. Wilshusen:

Thank you for the opportunity to comment on the Government Accountability Office (GAO) draft report entitled, *Social Media: Federal Agencies Need Policies and Procedures for Managing and Protecting Information They Access and Disseminate* (GAO-11-605).

The Department of Housing and Urban Development (HUD) reviewed the draft report and concurs with the following recommendation for executive action:

To ensure that appropriate security measures are in place when commercially provided social media services are used, we recommend that the Secretary of Housing and Urban Development take the following action.

- Conduct and document a security risk assessment to assess security threats associated with agency use of Twitter and YouTube and identify security controls that can be used to mitigate the identified threats.

HUD complied with the recommendation by conducting security risk assessments on agency use of Twitter and YouTube. The enclosed documentation will verify that appropriate security controls are in place to mitigate identified risks.

If you have any questions or require additional information, please contact Joyce M. Little, Director, Office of Investment Strategies Policy and Management at (202) 402-7404.

Sincerely,

Jerry E. Williams
Chief Information Officer

Enclosures

The following are GAO's comments to the Department of Housing and Urban Development's letter dated May 27, 2011.

GAO Comments

1. After reviewing the additional documentation provided, we updated our report to indicate that the department asserted that it is taking actions to conduct and document a security risk assessment related to its use of social media. We confirmed these actions.

APPENDIX XII. COMMENTS FROM THE DEPARTMENT OF VETERANS AFFAIRS

Note: GAO's comments supplementing those in the report's text appear at the end of this appendix.

DEPARTMENT OF VETERANS AFFAIRS
Washington DC 20420

May 31, 2011

Mr. Randall B. Williamson
Director, Health Care
U.S. Government Accountability Office
441 G Street, NW
Washington, DC 20548

Dear Mr. Williamson:

The Department of Veterans Affairs (VA) has reviewed the Government Accountability Office's (GAO) draft report, *"SOCIAL MEDIA: Federal Agencies Need Policies and Procedures for Managing and Protecting Information They Access and Disseminate"* (GAO-11-605), and generally agrees with GAO's conclusions and concurs with GAO's recommendations to the Department.

The enclosure specifically addresses GAO's recommendations and provides comments to the report. VA appreciates the opportunity to comment on your draft report.

Sincerely,

John R. Gingrich
Chief of Staff

Enclosure

See comment 1. See comment 2.

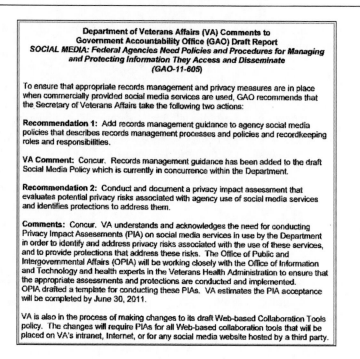

Department of Veterans Affairs (VA) Comments to Government Accountability Office (GAO) Draft Report
SOCIAL MEDIA: Federal Agencies Need Policies and Procedures for Managing and Protecting Information They Access and Disseminate
(GAO-11-605)

To ensure that appropriate records management and privacy measures are in place when commercially provided social media services are used, GAO recommends that the Secretary of Veterans Affairs take the following two actions:

Recommendation 1: Add records management guidance to agency social media policies that describes records management processes and policies and recordkeeping roles and responsibilities.

VA Comment: Concur. Records management guidance has been added to the draft Social Media Policy which is currently in concurrence within the Department.

Recommendation 2: Conduct and document a privacy impact assessment that evaluates potential privacy risks associated with agency use of social media services and identifies protections to address them.

Comments: Concur. VA understands and acknowledges the need for conducting Privacy Impact Assessments (PIA) on social media services in use by the Department in order to identify and address privacy risks associated with the use of these services, and to provide protections that address these risks. The Office of Public and Intergovernmental Affairs (OPIA) will be working closely with the Office of Information and Technology and health experts in the Veterans Health Administration to ensure that the appropriate assessments and protections are conducted and implemented. OPIA drafted a template for conducting these PIAs. VA estimates the PIA acceptance will be completed by June 30, 2011.

VA is also in the process of making changes to its draft Web-based Collaboration Tools policy. The changes will require PIAs for all Web-based collaboration tools that will be placed on VA's intranet, Internet, or for any social media website hosted by a third party.

The following are GAO's comments to the Department of Veterans Affairs' letter dated May 31, 2011.

GAO Comments

1. After reviewing additional comments provided by department representatives, we updated our report to indicate that the department asserted that it is taking actions to develop records management guidance for social media use, although the guidance has not yet been finalized. We have not evaluated these actions.

2. After reviewing additional comments provided by department representatives, we updated our report to indicate that the department asserted that it is taking actions to develop a PIA for its social media use, although the PIA has not yet been finalized. We have not evaluated these actions.

APPENDIX XIII. COMMENTS FROM THE ENVIRONMENTAL PROTECTION AGENCY

Note: GAO's comments supplementing those in the report's text appear at the end of this appendix.

UNITED STATES ENVIRONMENTAL PROTECTION AGENCY
WASHINGTON, D.C. 20460

MAY 2 5 2011

OFFICE OF
ENVIRONMENTAL INFORMATION

Mr. Gregory C. Wilshusen
Director
Information Security Issues
U.S. Government Accountability Office
441 G Street, NW
Washington, DC 20548

Re: EPA Comments on the Government Accountability Office's (GAO) draft report
entitled *Social Media: Federal Agencies Need Policies and Procedures for
Managing and Protecting Information They Access and Disseminate (GAO-11-605)*

Dear Mr. Wilshusen:

This letter provides the U.S. Environmental Protection Agency's (EPA) comments
on GAO's draft report entitled *Social Media: Federal Agencies Need Policies and
Procedures for Managing and Protecting Information They Access and Disseminate
(GAO-11-605)*. EPA appreciates the review GAO has conducted with 24 major agencies,
as well as the opportunity to provide comments on this draft report.

EPA understands the importance of access to its environmental information and is
fully committed to using social media to make its information available to an even wider
audience. This is a timely GAO report as social media offers many exciting
opportunities, while at the same time creating special challenges for federal agencies.

Here at EPA, we understand the need to provide our staff with policies,
procedures and guidance as they continue to implement social media. With the need to
ensure that proper records are maintained, that privacy is protected, and that EPA's
information systems are protected from security threats and risks, it is vital that EPA have
clear processes in place to address these issues. EPA is currently in the final stages of
completing the Social Media Policy along with three accompanying procedures: Using
Social Media Internally at EPA, Using Social Media to Communicate with the Public,
and Representing EPA Online Using Social Media.

EPA appreciates the recommendations set forth in the GAO draft report. As we
continue to move forward with the use of social media, the Agency has made these
recommendations a priority.

I have enclosed our specific technical comments to the GAO recommendations.
If you would like to discuss these matters further, please contact me at 202-564-6665, or
your staff may contact Todd Holderman, Director of the Information Access Division, at
202-564-8598.

Sincerely,

Malcolm D. Jackson
Assistant Administrator
and Chief Information Officer

See comment 1.
See comment 2.

EPA's Response to GAO Recommendations

ENVIRONMENTAL PROTECTION AGENCY: Draft GAO Report (GAO-11-605):
Social Media: *Federal Agencies Need Policies and Procedures for Managing and Protecting Information They Access and Disseminate.*

Lead Office: Office of Environmental Information

Participating Offices: Office of Information Analysis and Access, Office of Information Collection, and the Office of External Affairs and Environmental Education.

GAO Recommendation

Conduct and document a privacy impact assessment that evaluates potential privacy risks associated with agency use of social media services and identifies protections to address them.

EPA Response

> EPA agrees. The Agency's Office of External Affairs and Environmental Education (OEAEE) is responsible for the planning, development and review of all Agency web products intended for the public and targeted audiences. OEAEE will conduct a privacy impact assessment (PIA) of EPA's use of social media services and identify protections to mitigate any risks identified. The PIA will be completed by June 30, 2011.

GAO Recommendation

Conduct and document a security risk assessment to assess security threats associated with agency use of commercially provided social media services and identify security controls that can be used to mitigate the identified threats.

EPA Response

> EPA agrees. The Environmental Protection Agency (EPA) will assess risks associated with commercially provided social media services we use. Risks will be assessed by identifying associated threats and vulnerabilities and evaluating them against likelihood of occurrence and adverse impact. We will identify proper security controls that can be used to mitigate identified risks to an acceptable level. The risk assessment will be completed by June 1, 2012.

The following are GAO's comments to the Environmental Protection Agency's letter dated May 25, 2011.

GAO Comments

1. After reviewing additional comments provided by agency representatives, we updated our report to indicate that the agency asserted that it is taking actions to develop a PIA for its social media use, although the PIA has not yet been finalized. We have not evaluated these actions.

2. After reviewing additional comments provided by agency representatives, we updated our report to indicate that the agency asserted taking actions to develop a security risk assessment for social media use, although the assessment has not yet been finalized. We have not evaluated these actions.

APPENDIX XIV. COMMENTS FROM THE NATIONAL AERONAUTICS AND SPACE ADMINISTRATION

The following are GAO's comments to the National Aeronautics and Space Administration's letter dated May 31, 2011.

GAO Comments

1. After reviewing additional efforts stated by the agency, we updated our report to indicate that the agency has plans to develop privacy policies addressing the agency's use of PII made available through social media services.

2. After reviewing additional comments provided by agency representatives, we updated our report to indicate that the agency asserted that it is taking actions to develop a PIA for its social media use, although the PIA has not yet been finalized. We have not evaluated these actions.

3. After reviewing additional comments provided by agency representatives, we updated our report to indicate that the agency asserted that it is taking actions to develop a security risk assessment for social media use, although the assessment has not yet been finalized. We have not evaluated these actions.

See comment 1. See comment 2.

National Aeronautics and Space Administration

Headquarters
Washington, DC 20546-0001

MAY 31 2011

Reply to Attn of:

Office of the Chief Information Officer

Mr. Gregory C. Wilshusen
Director, Information Security Issues
United States Government Accountability Office
Washington, DC 20548

Dear Mr. Wilshusen:

The National Aeronautics and Space Administration (NASA) appreciates the opportunity to review and comment on your draft report entitled, "Social Media: Federal Agencies Need Policies and Procedures for Managing and Protecting Information They Access and Disseminate" (GAO-11-605). In the draft report, GAO makes three recommendations to ensure that appropriate privacy and security measures are in place when commercially provided social media services are used by NASA, specifically:

Recommendation 1: The Administrator of the National Aeronautics and Space Administration update privacy policies to describe whether PII made available through use of social media services is collected and used.

Management Response: NASA concurs with the GAO recommendation. The NASA Chief Information Officer (CIO) has already disseminated guidance regarding privacy implications in the use of social media through a CIO memorandum on "Appropriate Use of Web Technologies," issued August 12, 2010, through an Agency-wide user notification and through the NASA CIO Web site. In addition, NASA has been reviewing all agency privacy policies and will update these policies to address appropriate security measures, prohibitions, and controls required for the use of social media services.

Recommendation 2: The Administrator of the National Aeronautics and Space Administration conduct and document a privacy impact assessment that evaluates potential privacy risks associated with agency use of social media services and identifies protections to address them.

Management Response: NASA concurs with the GAO recommendation. NASA policy requires that Information and Privacy Threshold Analyses (IPTAs), and, if appropriate, full Privacy Impact Assessments (PIAs), be conducted on all known systems. However, the data generated or collected by the social media services within the scope of this GAO engagement (Facebook, YouTube, Twitter) exist outside of the NASA enterprise architecture and administrative control. As previously reported to GAO on

See comment 3.

January 10, 2011, no personally identifiable information is collected from comments posted by the public on NASA's own Facebook, YouTube, and Twitter pages. Nevertheless, NASA is currently developing a PIA of these social media services in accordance with OMB Memorandum 10-23, which requires an adapted PIA whenever an Agency's use of a third-party Web site or application makes PII available to the Agency. Using all information available to NASA, this PIA will evaluate potential privacy risks and identify every possible protection to address these risks.

Recommendation 3: The Administrator of the National Aeronautics and Space Administration conduct and document a security risk assessment to assess security threats associated with agency use of commercially provided social media services and identify security controls that can be used to mitigate the identified threats.

Management Response: NASA concurs with the GAO recommendation. NASA is conducting and documenting a security risk assessment to assess security threats associated with Agency use of commercially provided social media services, which will identify or verify common security controls. In addition, NASA periodically reviews the security posture of commercial social media products for new vulnerabilities and updates its infrastructure or procedures accordingly. NASA has also added social media risks to the Agency's risk profile and updated information security training to educate its community on the risks associated with commercial social media services.

If you have any questions or require additional information, please contact the NASA Deputy CIO for IT Security, Valarie Burks at (202) 358-3716.

Sincerely,

Linda Cureton
Chief Information Officer

APPENDIX XV.
COMMENTS FROM THE OFFICE
OF PERSONNEL MANAGEMENT

Note: GAO's comments supplementing those in the report's text appear at the end of this appendix.

See comment 1.

UNITED STATES OFFICE OF PERSONNEL MANAGEMENT
Washington, DC 20415

Chief Information
Officer

May 24, 2011

Mr. Gregory C. Wilshusen, Director
Information Security Issues
U.S. Government Accountability Office
441 G Street, N.W.
Washington, DC 20548

Dear Mr. Wilshusen:

We recognize that even the most well run programs can benefit from an external evaluation and we appreciate the input of the Government Accountability Office as we continue to enhance our social media program. We have reviewed your draft audit report (GAO-11-605) titled Social Media: Federal Agencies Need Policies and Procedures for Managing and Protecting Information and are in concurrence with the two recommendations for Office of Personnel Management (OPM) identified in the report. Specific responses to your recommendations are provided below.

Response to Recommendations

RECOMMENDATION: To ensure that appropriate privacy and security measures are in place when commercially provided social media services are used, we recommend that the Director of the OPM take the following two actions:

- Conduct and document a privacy impact assessment that evaluates potential privacy risks associated with agency use of social media services and identifies protections to address them.
- Conduct and document a security risk assessment to assess security threats associated with agency use of commercially provided social media services and identify security controls that can be used to mitigate the identified threats.

MANAGEMENT RESPONSE: Concur. OPM shall conduct a privacy impact assessment and a security risk assessment as stated in the recommendation. We will complete these assessments no later than September 30, 2011.

Sincerely,

Matthew E. Perry
Chief Information Officer

The following are GAO's comments to the Office of Personnel Management's letter dated May 24, 2011.

GAO Comments

1. After reviewing additional comments and materials provided by agency representatives, we updated our report to indicate that the agency asserted that it is taking actions to develop both a PIA and a security risk assessment for its social media use. We have not evaluated these actions.

APPENDIX XVI.
COMMENTSFROM THE SOCIAL SECURITY ADMINISTRATION

Note: GAO's comments supplementing those in the report's text appear at the end of this appendix.

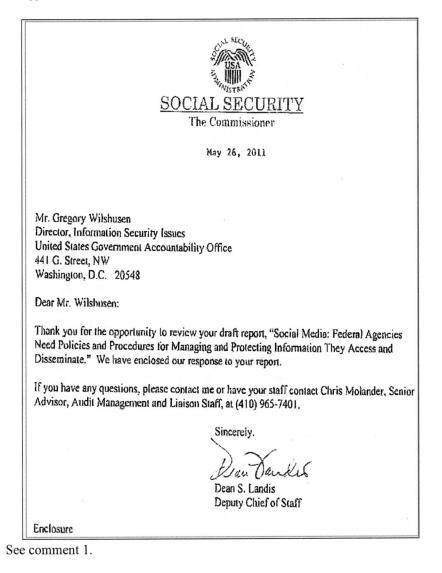

SOCIAL SECURITY

The Commissioner

May 26, 2011

Mr. Gregory Wilshusen
Director, Information Security Issues
United States Government Accountability Office
441 G. Street, NW
Washington, D.C. 20548

Dear Mr. Wilshusen:

Thank you for the opportunity to review your draft report, "Social Media: Federal Agencies Need Policies and Procedures for Managing and Protecting Information They Access and Disseminate." We have enclosed our response to your report.

If you have any questions, please contact me or have your staff contact Chris Molander, Senior Advisor, Audit Management and Liaison Staff, at (410) 965-7401.

Sincerely.

Dean S. Landis
Deputy Chief of Staff

Enclosure

See comment 1.

SOCIAL SECURITY ADMINISTRATION COMMENTS ON THE GOVERNMENT ACCOUNTABILITY OFFICE DRAFT REPORT, "SOCIAL MEDIA: FEDERAL AGENCIES NEED POLICIES AND PROCEDURES FOR MANAGING AND PROTECTING INFORMATION THEY ACCESS AND DISSEMINATE" (GAO-11-605)

We offer the following comment.

Recommendation

To ensure that appropriate privacy measures are in place when commercially provided social media services are used, we recommend that the Commissioner of the Social Security Administration take the following action.

• Update privacy policies to describe whether PII made available through use of social media services is collected and used.

Response

We do not use or collect PII made available through social media services. However, we will update our privacy policy to reflect that fact and post the update to our agency website.

The following are GAO's comments to the Social Security Administration's letter dated May 26, 2011.

GAO Comments

1. After reviewing additional comments stated by the agency, we updated our report to indicate that the agency has plans to develop privacy policies addressing the agency's use of PII made available through social media services.

APPENDIX XVII. COMMENTS FROM THE U.S. AGENCY FOR INTERNATIONAL DEVELOPMENT

Note: GAO's comments supplementing those in the report's text appear at the end of this appendix.

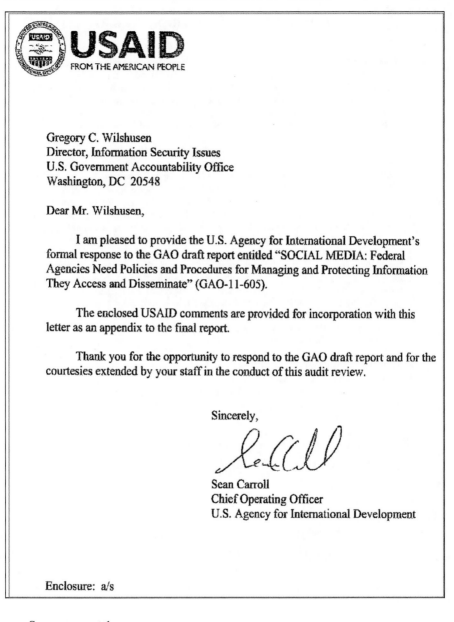

USAID

FROM THE AMERICAN PEOPLE

Gregory C. Wilshusen
Director, Information Security Issues
U.S. Government Accountability Office
Washington, DC 20548

Dear Mr. Wilshusen,

I am pleased to provide the U.S. Agency for International Development's formal response to the GAO draft report entitled "SOCIAL MEDIA: Federal Agencies Need Policies and Procedures for Managing and Protecting Information They Access and Disseminate" (GAO-11-605).

The enclosed USAID comments are provided for incorporation with this letter as an appendix to the final report.

Thank you for the opportunity to respond to the GAO draft report and for the courtesies extended by your staff in the conduct of this audit review.

Sincerely,

Sean Carroll
Chief Operating Officer
U.S. Agency for International Development

Enclosure: a/s

See comment 1.
See comment 2.

USAID COMMENTS ON GAO DRAFT REPORT No. GAO-11-605

Recommendation 1: To ensure that appropriate records management and security measures are in place when commercially provided social media services are used, we recommend that the Administrator of the U.S. Agency for International Development (USAID) take the following action: Add records management guidance to agency social media policies that describes records management processes and policies and recordkeeping roles and responsibilities.

Response: USAID concurs with recommendation 1. USAID recognizes the importance of adding sound records management guidance to the agency's social media policies. The Information and Records Division in the Bureau for Management's Office of Management Services is currently reviewing the various social media activities in which the agency is involved, and will establish records management guidance that will effectively apply lifecycle management and appropriate records disposition authority to the electronic record content published by USAID on social media sites. Target Completion Date: December 31, 2011

Recommendation 2: To ensure that appropriate records management and security measures are in place when commercially provided social media services are used, we recommend that the Administrator of the U.S. Agency for International Development take the following action, conduct and document a security risk assessment to assess security threats associated with agency use of commercially provided social media services and identify security controls that can be used to mitigate the identified threats.

Response: The Chief Information Security Officer (CISO) concurs with recommendation 2. CISO will conduct a full risk assessment, identify security controls or compensating controls and/or create a plan of action and milestones where necessary. Target Completion Date: June 3, 2011.

The following are GAO's comments to the U.S. Agency for International Development's letter received on May 27, 2011.

GAO Comments

1. After reviewing additional comments provided by agency representatives, we updated our report to indicate that the agency asserted that it is taking actions to develop records management guidance for social media use. We have not evaluated these actions.

2. After reviewing additional comments provided by agency representatives, we updated our report to indicate that the agency asserted that it is taking actions to develop a security risk assessment for social media use, although the assessment has not yet been finalized. We have not evaluated these actions.

End Notes

[1] The White House, *Memorandum for the Heads of Executive Departments and Agencies: Transparency and Open Government* (Washington, D.C.: Jan. 21, 2009).

[2] For purposes of this report, the terms personal information and personally identifiable information are used interchangeably to refer to any information about an individual maintained by an agency, including (1) any information that can be used to distinguish or trace an individual's identity, such as name, Social Security number, date and place of birth, mother's maiden name, or biometric records, and (2) any other information that is linked or linkable to an individual, such as medical, educational, financial, and employment information.

[3] The 24 major departments and agencies are the Departments of Agriculture, Commerce, Defense, Education, Energy, Health and Human Services, Homeland Security, Housing and Urban Development, the Interior, Justice, Labor, State, Transportation, the Treasury, and Veterans Affairs; the Environmental Protection Agency, General Services Administration, National Aeronautics and Space Administration, National Science Foundation, Nuclear Regulatory Commission, Office of Personnel Management, Small Business Administration, Social Security Administration, and U.S. Agency for International Development.

[4] We selected Facebook, Twitter, and YouTube because of their widespread use within the federal government as well as their broad popularity with the public.

[5] Because the Nuclear Regulatory Commission (NRC) did not use Facebook, Twitter, or YouTube at the time of our review, we did not include it as part of our evaluation.

[6] Chartered by Congress in 1967 as an independent, non-partisan organization, the National Academy is a non-profit, independent coalition of public management and organizational leaders that provides insights on key public management issues and advisory services to government agencies.

[7] The Nielsen Company is a global information and measurement company in marketing and consumer information, television and other media measurement, online intelligence, mobile measurement, trade shows, and related assets. The company has a presence in approximately 100 countries, with headquarters in New York.

[8] An administrator of a YouTube page can elect to remove the ability for users to leave comments.

[9] The Nuclear Regulatory Commission (NRC) does not use Facebook, YouTube, or Twitter.

[10] National Archives and Records Administration, Bulletin 2011-02: *Guidance on Managing Records in Web 2.0/Social Media Platforms* (College Park, Md.: Oct. 20, 2010).

[11] Office of Management and Budget, Memorandum M-10-23: *Guidance for Agency Use of Third-Party Websites and Applications* (Washington, D.C.: June 25, 2010).

[12] NIST, *Recommended Security Controls for Federal Information Systems and Organizations*, Special Publication 800-53, Revision 3 (Gaithersburg, Md.: August 2009).

[13] GAO, *Information Management: Challenges in Federal Agencies' Use of Web 2.0 Technologies*, GAO-10-872 T (Washington, D.C.: July 22, 2010).

[14] Director of National Intelligence, Statement for the Record on the Worldwide Threat Assessment of the U.S. Intelligence Community, statement before the Senate Select Committee on Intelligence (Feb. 16, 2011).

[15] Federal Trade Commission, FTC Accepts Final Settlement with Twitter for Failure to Safeguard Personal Information (press release, Mar. 11, 2011), http://www.ftc.gov/opa/2011/03/twitter.shtm.

[16] We reviewed agency use of these services from July 2010 through January 2011. Because the Nuclear Regulatory Commission (NRC) did not use any of the three social media services, we did not include it in our evaluation.

[17] Twitter differs from the other two social media services in that comments received to a Twitter account are not visible on the account's Twitter page. A tweet in reply to a comment

received is indicated by including the "@" symbol and the user name of the original commenter.

[18] GAO-10-872T.

[19] The 12 agencies with records management guidance are the Departments of Commerce, Defense, Energy, Health and Human Services, Housing and Urban Development, the Interior, Justice, Labor, State, and Transportation; the Environmental Protection Agency; and the General Services Administration.

[20] During the course of our review, 8 agencies reported taking actions to develop records management guidance that were not yet complete: the Departments of Agriculture, Education, Homeland Security, and the Treasury; National Aeronautics and Space Administration; Office of Personnel Management; Small Business Administration, and Social Security Administration. Two additional agencies that had not previously provided information about actions to develop records management guidance did so in comments on a draft of this report. Those agencies included the Department of Veterans Affairs and the U.S. Agency for International Development.

[21] National Archives and Records Administration: *A Report of Federal Web 2.0 Use and Record Value* (Sept. 1, 2010).

[22] GAO-10-872T.

[23] GAO-10-872T.

[24] "Making PII available" includes any agency action that causes PII to become available or accessible to the agency, whether or not the agency solicits or collects it.

[25] The 12 agencies with updated privacy policies were the Departments of Agriculture, Defense, Energy, Homeland Security, Housing and Urban Development, the Interior, Justice, State, and the Treasury; the Environmental Protection Agency; the National Science Foundation; and the Office of Personnel Management.

[26] During the course of our review, three agencies reported taking actions to initiate updates to their privacy policies although the policies had not yet been changed. These included the Department of Veterans Affairs, Small Business Administration, and U.S. Agency for International Development. Two additional agencies that had not previously provided information about actions to update their privacy policies did so in comments on a draft of this report. Those agencies included the Department of Education and General Services Administration.

[27] Eight agencies completed PIAs that apply to the use of Facebook, Twitter, and YouTube: the Departments of Energy, Homeland Security, Housing and Urban Development, the Interior, Justice, Labor, and Transportation; and the National Science Foundation.

[28] During the course of our review, five agencies reported taking actions to conduct and document PIAs that were not yet complete: the Departments of Commerce, Education, Health and Human Services; Social Security Administration; and U.S. Agency for International Development. Five additional agencies that had not previously provided information about actions to conduct and document PIAs did so in comments on a draft of this report. Those agencies included the Departments of Defense and Veterans Affairs; Environmental Protection Agency; National Aeronautics and Space Administration; and Office of Personnel Management.

[29] NIST, *Guide for Applying the Risk Management Framework to Federal Information Systems*, Special Publication 800-37, Revision 1 (Gaithersburg, Md.: February 2010).

[30] NIST Special Publication 800-53, Revision 3.

[31] Seven agencies completed security risk assessments for Facebook, Twitter, and YouTube: the Departments of Agriculture, Defense, Health and Human Services, the Interior, Labor, and Veterans Affairs; and the General Services Administration.

[32] During the course of our review, 6 agencies reported taking actions to conduct and document security risk assessments that were not yet complete: the Departments of Education, Justice, and the Treasury; Environmental Protection Agency; Small Business Administration; and Social Security Administration. Six additional agencies that had not previously provided

information about actions to conduct and document assessments did so in comments on a draft of this report. Those agencies included the Departments of Energy, Homeland Security, and Housing and Urban Development; the National Aeronautical and Space Administration; the Office of Personnel Management; and the U.S. Agency for International Development.

[33] The agencies that included information on actions taken to address requirements within comments on a draft of this report were the Departments of Agriculture, Defense, Education, Energy, Homeland Security, Housing and Urban Development, State, the Treasury, and Veterans Affairs; the Environmental Protection Agency; the General Services Administration; the National Aeronautics and Space Administration; the Office of Personnel Management; the Small Business Administration; and the U.S. Agency for International Development.

[34] The 24 major departments and agencies are the Departments of Agriculture, Commerce, Defense, Education, Energy, Health and Human Services, Homeland Security, Housing and Urban Development, the Interior, Justice, Labor, State, Transportation, the Treasury, and Veterans Affairs; the Environmental Protection Agency, General Services Administration, National Aeronautics and Space Administration, National Science Foundation, Nuclear Regulatory Commission, Office of Personnel Management, Small Business Administration, Social Security Administration, and U.S. Agency for International Development.

[35] At the time of our review, the Nuclear Regulatory Commission (NRC) did not use Facebook, Twitter, or YouTube. Additionally, the Department of Health and Human Services did not maintain a Facebook page to represent its headquarters, although various components of HHS maintained their own Facebook pages.

[36] Because NRC did not use Facebook, Twitter, or YouTube at the time of our review, we did not include it in our evaluation of social media policies and procedures.

In: Social Media Use …   ISBN: 978-1-62100-747-0
Editor: Michael N. Brander   © 2012 Nova Science Publishers, Inc.

Chapter 2

INFORMATION MANAGEMENT CHALLENGES IN FEDERAL AGENCIES' USE OF WEB 2.0 TECHNOLOGIES[*]

Gregory C. Wilshusen

WHY GAO DID THIS STUDY

"Web 2.0" technologies—such as Web logs ("blogs"), social networking Web sites, video- and multimedia-sharing sites, and "wikis"—are increasingly being utilized by federal agencies to communicate with the public. These tools have the potential to, among other things, better include the public in the governing process. However, agency use of these technologies can present risks associated with properly managing and protecting government records and sensitive information, including personally identifiable information. In light of the rapidly increasing popularity of Web 2.0 technologies, GAO was asked to identify and describe current uses of Web 2.0 technologies by federal agencies and key challenges associated with their use.

To accomplish this, GAO analyzed federal policies, reports, and guidance related to the use of Web 2.0 technologies and interviewed officials at selected

---

[*] This is an edited, reformatted and augmented version of a Testimony before the Subcommittee on Information Policy, Census, and National Archives, Committee on Oversight and Government Reform, House of Representatives, GAO-10-872T dated July 22, 2010.

federal agencies, including the Department of Homeland Security, the General Services Administration, and the National Archives and Records Administration.

WHAT GAO FOUND

Federal agencies are using Web 2.0 technologies to enhance services and support their individual missions. Federal Web managers use these applications to connect to people in new ways. As of July 2010, we identified that 22 of 24 major federal agencies had a presence on Facebook, Twitter, and YouTube.

Several challenges in federal agencies' use of Web 2.0 technologies have been identified:

Privacy and security. Agencies are faced with the challenges of determining how the Privacy Act of 1974, which provides certain protections to personally identifiable information, applies to information exchanged in the use of Web 2.0 technologies, such as social networking sites. Further, the federal government may face challenges in determining how to appropriately limit collection and use of personal information as agencies utilize these technologies and how and when to extend privacy protections to information collected and used by third-party providers of Web 2.0 services. In addition, personal information needs to be safeguarded from security threats, and guidance may be needed for employees on how to use social media Web sites properly and how to handle personal information in the context of social media.

Records management and freedom of information. Web 2.0 technologies raise issues in the government's ability to identify and preserve federal records. Agencies may face challenges in assessing whether the information they generate and receive by means of these technologies constitutes federal records and establish mechanisms for preserving such records, which involves, among other things, determining the appropriate intervals at which to capture constantly changing Web content. The use of Web 2.0 technologies can also present challenges in appropriately responding to Freedom of Information Act (FOIA) requests because there are significant complexities in determining whether agencies control Web 2.0-generated content, as understood within the context of FOIA.

Federal agencies have begun to identify some of the issues associated with Web 2.0 technologies and have taken steps to start addressing them. For example, the Office of Management and Budget recently issued guidance intended to (1) clarify when and how the Paperwork Reduction Act of 1995 applies to federal agency use of social media and Web-based interactive technologies; and (2) help federal agencies protect privacy when using third-party Web sites and applications.

Chairman Clay and Members of the Subcommittee:

Thank you for the opportunity to testify today on the use of "Web 2.0" technologies by federal government agencies and the challenges associated with the use of these technologies.

Federal agencies are increasingly using recently developed technologies (commonly referred to as "Web 2.0" technologies) that offer flexible, sophisticated capabilities for interaction with individuals, allowing agencies and the public to publish comments, photos, and videos directly on agency-sponsored Web pages. The use of these tools by federal agencies is growing tremendously, supported by initiatives from the administration, directives from government leaders, and demands from the public. These tools offer the potential to better include people in the governing process and may also contribute to accomplishing agency missions. However, agency use of these technologies also may present risks associated with properly managing and protecting government records and sensitive information, including personally identifiable information.

In this statement I will describe the current uses of Web 2.0 technologies by federal agencies, key challenges associated with their use of these technologies, and initial steps agencies have taken to address identified issues.

My testimony is based on our analysis of federal government policies, reports, and guidance related to the use of Web 2.0 technologies. To perform our analysis, we reviewed relevant reports produced by the Department of Homeland Security (DHS), General Services Administration (GSA), and National Archives and Records Administration (NARA). Based on our review of these reports, we identified potential challenges related to privacy, security, records management, and freedom of information. We interviewed agency officials involved in the development of these reports to validate the challenges identified in relevant reports and obtain their views regarding the extent to which government efforts are underway to address them. We conducted our work from February 2010 to July 2010 in accordance with all sections of GAO's Quality Assurance Framework that are relevant to our objectives. The framework requires that we plan and perform the engagement to obtain sufficient and appropriate evidence to meet our stated objectives and to discuss any limitations to our work. We believe that the information and data obtained, and the analysis conducted, provide a reasonable basis for any findings and conclusions in this product.

In addition, at your request, we are currently undertaking a more comprehensive review of the management and protection of information collected and maintained by commercial providers of social media on behalf of or in association with federal agencies.

BACKGROUND

Internet-based services using Web 2.0 technology have become increasingly popular. Web 2.0 technologies refer to a second generation of the World Wide Web as an enabling platform for Web-based communities of interest, collaboration, and interactive services. These technologies include Web logs (known as "blogs"), which allow individuals to respond online to agency notices and other postings; social-networking sites (such as Facebook and Twitter), which also facilitate informal sharing of information among agencies and individuals; video-sharing Web sites (such as YouTube), which allow users to discover, watch, and share originally created videos; "wikis," which allow individual users to directly collaborate on the content of Web pages; "podcasting," which allows users to download audio content; and "mashups," which are Web sites that combine content from multiple sources.

While in the past Internet usage concentrated on sites that provide online shopping opportunities and other services, according to the Nielsen Company, today video and social networking sites have moved to the forefront, becoming the two fastest growing types of Web sites in 2009, with 87 percent more users than in 2003. Furthermore, in February 2009, usage of social networking services reportedly exceeded Web-based e-mail usage for the first time. Similarly, the number of American users frequenting online video sites has more than tripled since 2003.

Some of the most popular Web 2.0 technologies in use today are social networking services, such as Facebook and Twitter.

Facebook is a social networking site that lets users create personal profiles describing themselves and then locate and connect with friends, co-workers, and others who share similar interests or who have common backgrounds. According to the Nielsen Company, Facebook was the number one global social networking site in December 2009 with 206.9 million unique visitors.

Twitter is a social networking and blogging site that allows users to share and receive information through short messages. According to the Nielsen Company, Twitter has been the fastest-growing social networking Web site in terms of unique visitors, increasing over 500 percent, from 2.7 million visitors in December 2008 to 18.1 million in December 2009.

Table 1. Current and Potential Uses of Web 2.0 in the Federal Government

Web 2.0 technology	Simplified definition	Examples of federal use	Potential for government
Blogs	Web sites where regular entries are made (such as in a journal or diary) and presented in reverse chronological order.	White House Blog; Department of State's Dipnote Blog; The Transportation Security Administration's Air Security Blog	Can provide government information to new audiences and encourage public conversations on government issues.
Social networking sites	Web sites that connect people through online communities. Users can establish pages with their profiles and find other people they know or look for other members with similar interests or affiliations.	USA.gov Facebook Page; NASA Spacebook and CoLab Program; EPA Facebook Group; State Department and Transportation Security Administration Twitter accounts	Can support public interaction in response to agency announcements.
Video and multimedia sharing	Web sites that use videos, images, and audio libraries to share information.	USA.gov Multimedia Library; NASA's YouTube Page	Can support public outreach, education, training, and other communication with online audiences.
Wikis	Collections of Web pages that encourage users to contribute or directly modify the content.	GSA's Intergovernmental Solutions Wiki; Intellipedia; Office of Management and Budget's USA spending.gov Wiki	Can support public collaboration, knowledge sharing, and input on government issues.
Podcasting	Publishing audio files on the Web so they can be downloaded onto computers or portable listening devices. Users can subscribe to a "feed" of new audio files and	White House podcasts; USA.gov Federal Podcast Library; Webcontent. gov podcasts; Census daily podcasts	Provide updates, coverage of live government deliberations, emergency response information, and how-to messages to the public.

Table 1. (Continued)

Web 2.0 technology	Simplified definition	Examples of federal use	Potential for government
	download them automatically as they are posted.		
Mashups	Web sites that combine content from multiple sources for an integrated experience.	USA Search; HUD's National Housing Locator System	Can support richer information sharing by integrating external data and expanding government reach.

Source: GAO analysis of USA.gov and GSA data.

FEDERAL AGENCIES ARE INCREASINGLY USING WEB 2.0 TECHNOLOGIES

Federal agencies are increasingly using Web 2.0 technologies to enhance services and interactions with the public. Federal Web managers use these applications to connect to people in new ways. As of July 2010, we identified that 22 of 24 major federal agencies[1] had a presence on Facebook, Twitter, and YouTube.[2]

Use of such technologies was endorsed in President Obama's January 2009 memorandum promoting transparency and open government.[3] The memorandum encouraged executive departments and agencies to harness new technologies to put information about their operations and decisions online so that it would be readily available to the public. It also encouraged the solicitation of public feedback to identify information of the greatest use to the public, assess and improve levels of collaboration, and identify new opportunities for cooperation in government. Table 1 presents examples of Web 2.0 technologies and their current uses in the federal government.

Federal agencies have been adapting Web 2.0 technologies to support their individual missions. For example:

- The U.S. Agency for International Development (USAID) uses Facebook to inform the public about the developmental and humanitarian assistance that it is providing to different countries in the world. It also posts links to other USAID resources, including blogs, videos, and relevant news articles.

- The National Aeronautics and Space Administration (NASA) uses Twitter to notify the public about the status of its missions as well as to respond to questions regarding space exploration. For example, NASA recently posted entries about its Mars Phoenix Lander mission on Twitter, which included answers to questions by individuals who followed its updates on the site.

- The State Department uses YouTube and other video technology in supporting its public diplomacy efforts. The department posts YouTube videos of remarks by Secretary Clinton, daily press briefings, interviews of U.S. diplomats, and testimonies by ambassadors. It also conducted a global video contest that encouraged public participation. The department then posted the videos submitted to it on its America.gov Web site to prompt further online discussion and participation.

- The Transportation Security Administration (TSA) developed a blog to facilitate an ongoing dialogue on security enhancements to the passenger screening process. The blog provides a forum for TSA to provide explanations about issues that can arise during the passenger screening process and describe the rationale for the agency's policies and practices. TSA also uses Twitter to alert subscribers to new blog posts. A program analyst in TSA's Office of Strategic Communications and Public Affairs stated that blogging encourages conversation, and provides direct and timely clarification regarding issues of public concern.

DETERMINING APPROPRIATE AGENCY USE OF WEB 2.0 TECHNOLOGIES PRESENTS CHALLENGES

While the use of Web 2.0 technologies can transform how federal agencies engage the public by allowing citizens to be more involved in the governing process, agency use of such technologies can also present challenges related to privacy, security, records management, and freedom of information.

Privacy and Security Challenges

Determining how the Privacy Act of 1974 applies to government use of social media. The Privacy Act of 1974[4] places limitations on agencies' collection, disclosure, and use of personal information maintained in systems of records. The act describes a "record" as any item, collection, or grouping of information about an individual that is maintained by an agency and contains his or her name or another personal identifier. It also defines "system of records" as a group of records under the control of any agency from which information is retrieved by the name of the individual or by an individual identifier.

However, because of the nature of Web 2.0 technologies, identifying how the act applies to the information exchanged is difficult. Some cases may be more clear-cut than others. For example, as noted by a participant discussing Web 2.0 challenges at a recent conference sponsored by DHS, the Privacy Act clearly applies to systems owned and operated by the government that make use of Web 2.0 technologies. Government agencies may also take advantage of commercial Web 2.0 offerings, in which case they are likely to have much less control over the systems that maintain and exchange information. For example, a government agency that chooses to establish a presence on a third party provider's service, such as Facebook, could have limited control over what is done with its information once posted on the electronic venue. Given this limited control, key officials we interviewed said they are unsure about the extent to which personal information that is exchanged in such forums is protected by the provisions of the Privacy Act.

Ensuring that agencies are taking appropriate steps to limit the collection and use of personal information through social media. Privacy could be compromised if clear limits are not set on how the government uses personal information to which it has access in social networking environments. Social networking sites, such as Facebook, encourage people to provide personal information that they intend to be used only for social purposes. Government agencies that participate in such sites may have access to this information and may need rules on how such information can be used. While such agencies cannot control what information may be captured by social networking sites, they can make determinations about what information they will collect and what to disclose. However, unless rules to guide their decisions are clear, agencies could handle information inconsistently. Individual privacy could be affected, depending upon whether and how government agencies collect or use personal information disclosed by individuals in interactive settings.

Extending privacy protections to the collection and use of personal information by third party providers. Individuals interacting with the government via Web 2.0 media may provide personal information for specific government purposes and may not understand that the information may be collected and stored by third-party commercial providers. It also may not be clear as to whose privacy policy applies when a third party manages content on a government agency Web site. Accordingly, agencies may need to be clear about the extent to which they make use of commercial providers and the providers' specific roles. Uncertainty about who has access to personal information provided through agency social networking sites could diminish individuals' willingness to express their views and otherwise interact with the government.

Safeguarding personal information from security threats that target Web 2.0 technologies. Federal government information systems have been targeted by persistent, pervasive, aggressive threats.[5] In addition, as the popularity of social media has grown, they have increasingly been targeted as well. Thus as agencies make use of Web 2.0 technologies, they face persistent, sophisticated threats targeting their own information as well as the personal information of individuals interacting with them. The rapid development of Web 2.0 technologies makes it challenging to keep up with the constantly evolving threats deployed against them and raises the risks associated with government participation in such technologies.

Further, the Federal Information Security Management Act[6] states that agencies are responsible for the security of information collected or maintained on their behalf and for information systems used or operated on their behalf. The extent to which FISMA makes federal agencies responsible for the security of third-party social media Web sites may depend on whether such sites are operating their systems or collecting information on behalf of the federal government, which may not be clear.

Training government participants on the proper use of social networking tools. Use of Web 2.0 technologies can result in a blending of professional and personal use by government employees, which can pose risks to their agencies. When an individual identifies him- or herself on a social media site as a federal employee, he or she provides information that may be exploited in a cyber attack on the agency. However, federal guidance may be needed for employees on how to use social media Web sites properly and how to handle personal information in the context of social media. In addition, training may be needed to ensure that employees are aware of agency policies and accountable for adhering to them.

Records Management and Freedom of Information Challenges

Determining requirements for preserving Web 2.0 information as federal records. A challenge associated with government use of Web 2.0 technologies, including government blogs and wikis and Web pages hosted by commercial providers, is the question of whether information exchanged through these technologies constitute federal records pursuant to the Federal Records Act.[7] The National Archives and Records Administration (NARA) has issued guidance to help agencies make decisions on what records generated by these technologies should be considered agency records. According to the guidance, records generated when a user interacts with an agency Web site may form part of a set of official agency records.[8] NARA guidance also indicates that content created with interactive software on government Web sites is owned by the government, not the individuals who created it, and is likely to constitute agency records and should be managed as such. Given these complex considerations, it may be challenging for federal agencies engaging the public via Web 2.0 technologies to assess the information they generate and receive via these technologies to determine its status as federal records.

Establishing mechanisms for preserving Web 2.0 information as records. Once the need to preserve information as federal records has been established, mechanisms need to be put in place to capture such records and preserve them properly. Proper records retention management needs to take into account NARA record scheduling requirements and federal law, which requires that the disposition of all federal records be planned according to an agency schedule or a general records schedule approved by NARA. The records schedule identifies records as being either temporary or permanent and sets times for their disposal.

These requirements may be challenging for agencies because the types of records involved when information is collected via Web 2.0 technologies may not be clear. For example, part of managing Web records includes determining when and how Web "snapshots" should be taken to capture the content of agency Web pages as they existed at particular points in time. Business needs and the extent to which unique information is at risk of being lost determine whether such snapshots are warranted and their frequency. NARA guidance requires that snapshots be taken each time a Web site changes significantly; thus, agencies may need to assess how frequently the information on their sites changes.

Comments by individuals on agency postings may need to be scheduled in addition to agency postings. In the case of a wiki, NARA guidance requires agencies to determine whether the collaborative wiki process should be scheduled along with the resulting final product. In addition, because a wiki depends on a collaborative community to provide content, agencies are required to make determinations about how much content is required to make the wiki significant or "authoritative" from a record perspective.

The potential complexity of these decisions and the resulting record-keeping requirements and processes can be daunting to agencies.

Ensuring proper adherence to the requirements of FOIA. Federal agencies' use of Web 2.0 technologies could pose challenges in appropriately responding to FOIA requests. Determining whether Web 2.0 records qualify as "agency records" under FOIA's definition is a complex question. FOIA's definition focuses on the extent to which the government controls the information in question. According to the Department of Justice's FOIA guidance, courts apply a four-part test to determine whether an agency exercises control over a record. They examine: (a) who created the record and the intent of the record creator; (b) whether the agency intended to relinquish control; (c) the agency's ability to use or dispose of the record; and (d) the extent to which the record is integrated into the agency's files. Agency "control" is also the predominant consideration in determining whether information generated or maintained by a government contractor is subject to FOIA's requirements. Given the complexity of these criteria, agencies may be challenged in making appropriate FOIA determinations about information generated or disseminated via Web 2.0 technologies. If not handled properly, such information may become unavailable for public access.

FEDERAL AGENCIES HAVE TAKEN STEPS TO IDENTIFY AND START ADDRESSING WEB 2.0 TECHNOLOGY ISSUES

As federal agencies have increasingly adopted Web 2.0 technologies, often by making use of commercially provided services, information technology officials have begun to consider the array of privacy, security, records management, and freedom of information issues that such usage poses. Once these issues are understood, measures can then be developed and implemented to address them. Several steps have been taken to identify these issues and to begin developing processes and procedures to address them:

- In June 2009, DHS hosted a two-day public workshop to discuss leading practices for the use of social media technologies to further the President's Transparency and Open Government Initiative. The workshop consisted of panels of academic, private-sector, and public-sector experts and included discussions on social media activities of federal agencies and the impact of those activities on privacy and security. In November 2009, DHS released a report summarizing the findings of the panels and highlighting potential solutions. According to a DHS official involved in coordinating the workshop, the array of issues raised during the workshop—which are reflected in the challenges I have discussed today—remain critically important to effective agency use of Web 2.0 technologies and have not yet been fully addressed across the government.
- NARA has issued guidance outlining issues related to the management of government information associated with Web 2.0 use. The agency recently released a brief document, *Implications of Recent Web Technologies for NARA Web Guidance*, as a supplement to its guidance to federal agencies on managing Web-based records. The document discusses Web technologies used by federal agencies— including Web portals, blogs, and wikis—and their impact on records management. NARA officials recognize that the guidance does not fully address more recent Web 2.0 technologies, and they said the agency is currently conducting a study of the impact of those technologies and plans to release additional guidance later this year.
- In April 2009, the General Services Administration announced that it had negotiated terms-of-service agreements with several social networking providers, including Facebook, MySpace, and YouTube.

The purpose of these agreements was to provide federal agencies with standardized vehicles for engaging these providers and to resolve legal concerns raised by following the terms and conditions generally used by the providers, which posed problems for federal agencies, including liability, endorsements, advertising, and freedom of information. As a result, other federal agencies can take advantage of these negotiated agreements when determining whether to use the providers' services.

- The Office of Management and Budget (OMB), in response to President Obama's January 2009 memorandum promoting transparency and open government, recently issued guidance intended to (1) clarify when and how the Paperwork Reduction Act of 1995 (PRA)[9] applies to federal agency use of social media and Web-based interactive technologies; and (2) help federal agencies protect privacy when using third-party Web sites and applications. Specifically, a memo issued in April 2010[10] explained that certain uses of social media and web-based interactive technologies would not be treated as "information collections" that would otherwise require review under the PRA. Such uses include many uses of wikis, the posting of comments, the conduct of certain contests, and the rating and ranking of posts or comments by Web site users. It also states that items collected by third party Web sites or platforms that are not collecting information on behalf of the federal government are not subject to the PRA.

In addition, a memorandum issued by OMB in June 2010[11] called for agencies to provide transparent privacy policies, individual notice, and a careful analysis of the privacy implications whenever they choose to use third-party technologies to engage with the public. The memo stated—among other things—that prior to using any third-party Web site or application, agencies should examine the third-party's privacy policy to evaluate the risks and determine whether it is appropriate for agency use. Further, if agencies post links on their Web sites that lead to third-party Web sites, they should notify users that they are being directed to non-government Web sites that may have privacy policies that differ from the agency's. In addition, the memo required agencies to complete a privacy impact assessment whenever an agency's use of a third-party Web site or application gives it access to personally identifiable information.

In summary, federal agencies are increasingly using Web 2.0 technologies to enhance services and interactions with the public, and such technologies have the potential to transform how federal agencies engage the public by allowing citizens to become more involved in the governing process and thus promoting transparency and collaboration. However, determining the appropriate use of these new technologies presents new potential challenges to the ability of agencies to protect the privacy and security of sensitive information, including personal information, shared by individuals interacting with the government and to the ability of agencies to manage, preserve, and make available official government records.

Agencies have taken steps to identify these issues and begun developing processes and procedures for addressing them. Until such procedures are in place, agencies will likely continue to face challenges in appropriately using Web 2.0 technologies. We have ongoing work to assess these actions.

Mr. Chairman, this concludes my statement. I would be happy to answer any questions you or other Members of the Subcommittee may have.

ABBREVIATIONS

DHS	Department of Homeland Security
FOIA	Freedom of Information Act
GSA	General Services Administration
NARA	National Archives and Records Administration
NASA	National Aeronautics and Space Administration
OMB	Office of Management and Budget
PRA	Paperwork Reduction Act of 1995
USAID	U.S Agency for International Development
TSA	Transportation Security Administration

End Notes

[1] The 24 major departments and agencies (agencies) are the Departments of Agriculture, Commerce, Defense, Education, Energy, Health and Human Services, Homeland Security, Housing and Urban Development, the Interior, Justice, Labor, State, Transportation, the Treasury, and Veterans Affairs; the Environmental Protection Agency, General Services Administration, National Aeronautics and Space Administration, National Science Foundation, Nuclear Regulatory Commission, Office of Personnel Management, Small Business Administration, Social Security Administration, and U.S. Agency for International Development.

[2] Totals include Facebook, Twitter, and YouTube pages that were readily accessible through official agency Web sites as of July 19, 2010. For each of these three social media services, the 22 agencies using them varied.

[3] The White House, *Memorandum for the Heads of Executive Departments and Agencies: Transparency and Open Government* (Washington, D.C.: Jan. 21, 2009).

[4] The Privacy Act of 1974 (5 U.S.C § 552a) serves as a key mechanism for controlling the collection, use, and disclosure of personally identifiable information within the federal government. The act also allows citizens to learn how their personal information is collected, maintained, used, and disseminated by the federal government.

[5] U.S. Government Accountability Office, *Cybersecurity: Continued Attention Is Needed to Protect Federal Information Systems from Evolving Threats*, GAO-10-834T (Washington, D.C.: Jun. 16, 2010).

[6] 44 USC 3544(a)(1).

[7] The act provides that "records" include "all books, papers, maps, photographs, machine readable materials, or other documentary materials, regardless of physical form or characteristics, made or received by an agency of the United States Government under Federal law or in connection with the transaction of public business and preserved or appropriate for preservation by that agency or its legitimate successor as evidence of the organization, functions, policies, decisions, procedures, operations, or other activities of the Government or because of the informational value of data in them." 44 U.S.C.§ 3301.

[8] The National Archives and Records Administration, *Implications of Recent Web Technologies for NARA Web Guidance* (posted September 30, 2006). See http://www.archives.gov/records-mgmt/initiatives/web-tech.html.

[9] 44 U.S.C. § 3501, et. seq.

[10] OMB, Office of Information and Regualtory Affairs, *Memorandum for the Heads of Executive Departments and Agencies, and Independent Regulatory Agencies: Social Media, Web-Based Interactive Technologies, and the Paperwork Reduction Act* (Washington, D.C.: April 7, 2010).

[11] OMB, *Memorandum for the Heads of Executive Departments and Agencies: Guidance for Agency Use of Third-Party Websites and Applications*, M-10-23 (Washington, D.C.: June 25, 2010).

In: Social Media Use ...
Editor: Michael N. Brander

Chapter 3

SOCIAL NETWORKING AND CONSTITUENT COMMUNICATIONS: MEMBER USE OF TWITTER DURING A TWO-MONTH PERIOD IN THE 111th CONGRESS*

*Matthew Eric Glassman, Jacob R. Straus,
and Colleen J. Shogan*

SUMMARY

Beginning with the widespread use of e-mail by Congress in the mid-1990's, the development of new electronic technologies has altered the traditional patterns of communication between Members of Congress and constituents. Many Members now use e-mail, official websites, blogs, YouTube channels, and Facebook pages to communicate with their constituents—technologies that were either non-existent or not widely available 15 years ago.

These technologies have arguably served to enhance the ability of Members of Congress to fulfill their representational duties by providing greater opportunities for communication between the Member and individual constituents, supporting the fundamental democratic role of spreading

---

* This is an edited, reformatted and augmented version of Congressional Research Service Report R41066, dated February 3, 2010.

information about public policy and government operations. In addition, electronic technology has reduced the marginal cost of constituent communications; unlike postal letters, Members can reach large numbers of constituents for a relatively small fixed cost. Despite these advantages, electronic communications have raised some concerns. Existing law and chamber regulations on the use of communication media such as the franking privilege have proven difficult to adapt to the new electronic technologies.

This report examines Member use of one specific new electronic communication medium: Twitter. After providing an overview and background of Twitter, the report analyzes patterns of Member use of Twitter during August and September 2009. This report is inherently a snapshot in time of a dynamic process. As with any new technology, the number of Members using Twitter and the patterns of use may change rapidly in short periods of time. Thus, the conclusions drawn from this data can not be easily generalized nor can these results be used to predict future behavior.

The data show that 205 Representatives and Senators are registered with Twitter (as of September 30, 2009) and issued a total of 7,078 "tweets" during the data collection period of August and September 2009. With approximately 38% of House Members and 39% of Senators registered with Twitter, Members sent an average of 116 tweets per day collectively.

Members' use of Twitter can be divided into eight categories: position taking, policy, district or state activities, official congressional action, personal, media, campaign activities, and other. The data suggest that the most frequent type of tweets were district or state tweets (24%), followed by policy tweets (23%), media tweets (14%), and position-taking tweets (14%).

INTRODUCTION

Beginning with the widespread use of e-mail by Congress in the mid-1990's, the development and adoption of new electronic technologies has altered the traditional patterns of communication between Members of Congress and constituents. Many Members now use e-mail, official websites, blogs, YouTube channels, and Facebook pages to communicate with their constituents—technologies that were either non-existent or not widely available 15 years ago.

These technologies have arguably served to enhance the ability of Members of Congress to fulfill their representational duties by providing greater opportunities for communication between the Member and individual constituents, supporting the fundamental democratic role of spreading information about public policy and government operations.[1] Electronic communications, however, have raised some concerns. Existing law and chamber regulations on the use of communication media such as the United States Postal Service have proven difficult to adapt to the new electronic technologies. In addition, electronic media could provide Members with the ability to easily communicate information traditionally sent to the district (or state) with non-constituents or non-U.S. residents.

This report examines Member use of one specific new electronic communication medium: Twitter. After providing an overview and background of Twitter, the report analyzes patterns of Member use of Twitter during August and September 2009.[2] This report is inherently a snapshot in time of a dynamic process. As with any new technology, the number of Members using Twitter and the patterns of use may change rapidly in short periods of time and undoubtedly will change over longer periods of time. Thus, the conclusions drawn from this data can not be easily generalized nor can these results be used to predict future behavior.

CONSTITUENT COMMUNICATION

Members of Congress have more choices and options available to communicate with constituents than they did 15 years ago. In addition to traditional modes of communication such as town-hall meetings, telephone calls, and postal mail, Members can now reach their constituents via e-mail, websites, tele-town halls, online videos, social networking sites, and other electronic-based communication applications.

The rise of such electronic communication has altered the traditional patterns of communication between Members and constituents. Although virtually all Members continue to use traditional modes of constituent communication, use of new communications technology is increasing.[3] For example, prior to 1995, there was virtually no e-mail traffic between Members and constituents.[4] In 2008, almost 200 million e-mails were sent to the House of Representatives, and a similar number were sent from House computers.[5] Member official websites, blogs, YouTube channels, and Facebook pages—all non-existent several years ago—also receive significant traffic.[6] Conversely, the amount of postal mail sent to Congress has dropped by more than 50% during the same time period.[7] In addition, electronic technology has reduced the marginal cost of constituent communications; unlike postal letters,

Members can reach large numbers of constituents for a relatively small fixed cost.[8]

Member use of electronic communications has raised several concerns. Some of these concerns are similar to those associated with traditional modes of constituent communications, such as the potential electoral advantage that the franking privilege—the ability to send official mail for free—may confer on incumbent Members.[9] Other issues, such as the use of third-party communication software platforms, are unique to the new electronic mediums.[10] In addition, existing law and chamber regulations on the use of communication media, such as the United States Postal Service, have proven difficult to apply directly to the new electronic technologies.[11]

TWITTER

Created in 2006 by developer Jack Dorsey as a tool to keep in touch with friends, Twitter is a web-based social networking service that allows users to send and read short messages.[12] Also considered a micro-blogging site, Twitter users send "tweets" of up to 140 characters. These tweets are displayed on an author's Twitter home page and on the pages of people subscribed to the RSS feed associated with the author's Twitter home page.[13]

Sending Tweets

Twitter enables individual users to post thoughts on any number of topics or activities. While Twitter use varies, it has been used by individuals and organizations to state opinions, promote events, and announce the release of products and services. Several legislative branch entities actively use Twitter to communicate with interested parties. These include the U.S. Government Accountability Office (GAO),[14] the Library of Congress (LOC),[15] the Government Printing Office (GPO),[16] and the Law Library of Congress.[17] In addition, Restaurant Associates, the House's food service vendor, uses Twitter to announce daily specials and events. Posting under the user name "ushrcafes," a typical tweet might look like this:

It's Panini Week in Cannon Cafe! Today's featured panini is Chicken Parmesan. Buy a panini and get a free 16oz fountain drink all week![18]

Because of the 140 character limit on tweets, Twitter messages are necessarily short. The brevity of the messages highlights the ease with which tweets can be quickly sent from mobile devices to followers around the world. The rapid transmission of information allows individuals and groups to communicate instantly without limitation of physical distance.

Following Twitter

Twitter allows individual users to "follow" other Twitter subscribers and read their tweets from the Twitter homepage. Individuals may choose to follow another Twitter account if they are interested in the information provided, are friends with the Twitter account holder, or if they are a "fan" of an activity or place. Following another user's Twitter account allows for almost instant access to his or her tweets. This can be useful if a follower is looking for a featured item or to better understand the activities of the person or group he or she is following. Individuals who "follow" an individual Twitter user can have instant access to tweets through devices such as a Blackberry, iPhone, or other similar mobile, internet-ready devices.

DATA ANALYSIS

This report analyzes the following questions related to Member use of Twitter:

- What proportion of Members are using Twitter?
- How often and when are Members using Twitter?
- How widely are Member tweets being followed?
- What are Members tweeting about?

Methodology

For August and September 2009, Members and Senators who were registered to use Twitter were tracked for their submissions. The website TweetCongress[19] was initially used to identify Members who were using Twitter. The list from TweetCongress was then cross-checked against a list of all Members and the Twitter search engine was used to verify that the correct and most current Twitter feed was being analyzed. The August and September time period included times when the House and Senate were in session and in recess.

Several caveats accompany the results presented. First, the analysis treats all Member tweets as structurally identical, because each individual tweet reveals no information about its genesis. In some cases, Members might be personally tweeting, whereas in others they are delegating Twitter responsibilities to their communications staff. CRS draws no distinction between the two. Second, some Members use Twitter as a communication medium in their official public capacity as Members, whereas others use Twitter as a communication medium for their campaign. Although there are important differences in the laws and chamber rules governing these two uses, CRS draws no distinction between the two in its analysis.

Finally, the analysis covers only two months of Member tweeting.[20] Therefore, it is inherently a snapshot in time of a dynamic process. As with any new technology, the number of Members using Twitter and the patterns of use may change rapidly in short periods of time. Thus, the conclusions drawn from this data can not be easily generalized nor can they be used to predict future behavior. They do, however, provide a glimpse into how Members are using a new communications technology to share their positions, policy preferences, and activities.

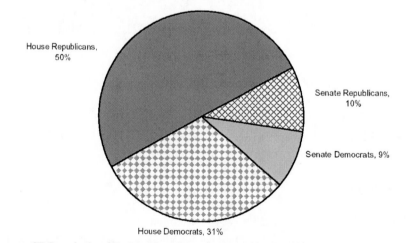

Source: CRS analysis of Twitter data from August 1 – September 30, 2009.

Figure 1. Chamber and Party Affiliation of Members Registered with Twitter As of September 30, 2009.

Results

A total of 7,078 tweets were sent by Members of Congress during the 61-day period between August 1, 2009, and September 30, 2009. During this period, the House was in session for 14 days and in recess for 47 days. The Senate was in session for 21 days and in recess for 40 days.

Member Registration with Twitter

As of September 30, 2009, a total of 205 Members of Congress were registered with Twitter, 39 Senators and 166 Representatives. Figure 1 presents the chamber and party affiliation of the 205 registered Members.

Although more than 80% of those registered were Representatives, registration rates were approximately equal between the chambers, with a slightly higher proportion of Senators (39%) registered than Representatives (38%).

Overall, 60% of registered Members were Republican and 40% were Democrats. As shown in Figure 1, approximately half of the Members registered with Twitter were Republican Members of the House of Representatives.

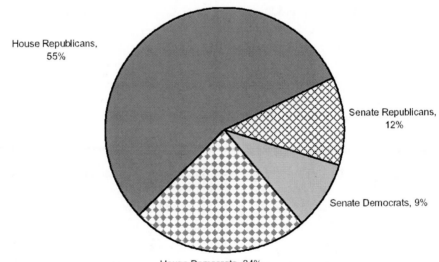

Source: CRS analysis of Twitter data from August 1 – September 30, 2009.

Figure 2. Proportion of Tweets Sent, by Chamber and Party Affiliation August 1- September 30, 2009.

Member Use of Twitter

Registration rates alone reveal little about actual Member *use* of Twitter, such as how often Members send tweets. During the two months of observation, registered Members sent a total of 7,078 tweets. The average number of tweets sent by an individual Member during the period was 35, or approximately one tweet every other day.

However, individual Member use of Twitter varied widely. The most active Member sent 291 tweets during the time period; several registered Members sent 0 tweets. Half of all registered Members sent 20 or fewer tweets during the time period; 16 Members sent more than 100 tweets.

Aggregated by chamber and party, Member use of Twitter was similar to Member registration rates. Seventy-nine percent (5,606) of all tweets were sent by Representatives, while 21% of all tweets (1,472) were sent by Senators. Figure 2 reports the percentage of tweets by chamber and party affiliation.

House Republicans sent approximately 55% of all tweets during the two-month period, while House Democrats sent 24% of all tweets. Senate Republicans sent slightly more tweets (12%) than Senate Democrats (9%).

While, in aggregate, a greater number of tweets were sent by Representatives than Senators and by Republicans than Democrats, this is in part because a greater number of Representatives and Republicans were registered for Twitter than Senators and Democrats, respectively. At the individual level, there was somewhat less variation. Among those registered for Twitter, the average Republican Senator sent slightly more tweets (39) than the average Democratic Senator (36) during the time period. The partisan variation was larger in the House. Registered Republican Representatives sent an average of 38 tweets during the time period, while the average number sent by registered Democratic Representatives was 27.

When Is Twitter Being Used?

Members sent a total of 7,078 tweets during August and September 2009, for an average of approximately 116 Member tweets per day. During this period, the House was in session for 14 days (and out of session for 47) and the Senate was in session for 21 days (and out of session for 40).

Overall, more tweets were sent during recess (3,772) than during session (3,356). However, Congress was on recess more than twice as many days as it was in session during the period under analysis. On a per-day basis, both Senators and Representatives sent significantly more tweets during session than during recess. Senators sent a total of 844 tweets in session, an average of 40 tweets per day. During recess, Senators sent a total 628 tweets, an average of 16 tweets a day. Representatives sent a total of 2,512 tweets in session, for an average of 179 tweets a day. During recess, Representatives sent a total of 3,094 tweets, for an average of 66 tweets a day.

The tendency toward in-session tweeting also contained a partisan component. Figure 3 reports the average number of tweets per day by party and chamber affiliation.

As shown in Figure 3, Members in both chambers and both parties sent significantly more tweets during session than during recess. However, the magnitude of the difference between session tweets and recess tweets was greater for Republican Representatives (approximately 3.0 times as many session tweets as recess tweets) and Democratic Senators (2.9) than for Democratic Representatives (2.2) and Republican Senators (2.3).

Data was also collected on the day of the week each Member tweet was sent. Figure 4 and Figure 5 report the average number of tweets sent by day of the week in the House and Senate, respectively, and whether the affiliated chamber was in session or recess.

As shown in Figure 4, Representative tweeting during recess was relatively uniform on the weekdays; no weekday had less than 84 tweets on average, and no weekday had more than 104 tweets on average. Representatives, however, were less likely to tweet on the weekends.

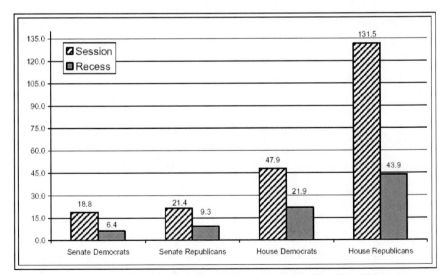

Source: CRS analysis of Twitter data from August 1 – September 30, 2009.

Figure 3. Average Tweets per Day, by Chamber and Party Affiliation August 1 – September 30, 2009.

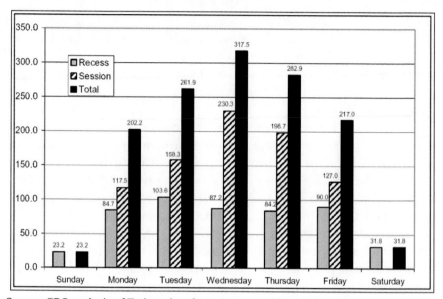

Source: CRS analysis of Twitter data from August and September, 2009.

Figure 4. Representative Tweets, Average Per Day of Week Includes In Session, Out of Session, and Total Tweets.

During session, Representatives sent the most tweets (an average of 230) on Wednesdays. Fewer tweets were sent, on average, on Mondays (118), Tuesdays (158), Thursdays (149), and Fridays (127). This perhaps reflects the general dynamics of House legislative activity when in session.

As shown in Figure 5, tweets by Senators followed a similar pattern to those of Representatives. Weekday tweeting during recess was relatively uniform, with no day averaging fewer than 18 tweets or more than 24. As with Representatives, Senators were less likely to tweet on the weekends. During session, Senators also sent the most tweets (an average of 57) on Wednesdays. Fewer tweets were sent, on average, on Mondays (30), Tuesdays (39), Thursdays (37), and Fridays (32).

What Are Members Tweeting About?

To assess the content of Member tweets, eight major message categories were hypothesized: position taking, policy statements, media or public relations, district or state, official or congressional action, personal, campaign, and other.[21] Each observed Member tweet was coded into one, and only one, category.

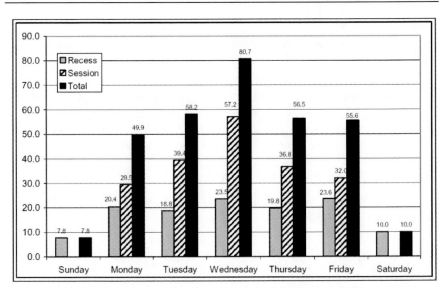

Source: CRS analysis of Twitter data from August and September, 2009.

Figure 5. Senator Tweets, Average Per Day of Week Includes In Session, Out of Session, and Total Tweets.

Each tweet was coded according to two main characteristics: who issued the tweet and the type of tweet issued. All tweets were coded according to the issuer's party affiliation and whether the Member serves in the House or the Senate. All tweets were also coded into discrete categories concerning the type of message issued. Each author coded approximately one-third of the 7,078 tweets collected. To maintain consistency in coding, inter-coder reliability was established by having each author code the same sample of tweets.

The categories were defined as follows:

Position Taking

Tweets in which a Representative or Senator took a position on a policy or political issue. The expressed position could concern a specific bill under consideration or a general policy issue.

Met with Bernanke this morning. Reiterated my support for S. 604, legislation to audit the Federal Reserve.[22]
Listened to the President tonight and what we need is a new bill, not a new speech. The problem isn't the messenger, it's the message.[23]

Policy Statement

Tweets in which a Representative or Senator discusses public policy without taking a position.

> White House: Cap and trade could cost families $1,761 a year http://tiny.cc/9gOUg[24]
> What is a health care exchange and how would health care reform affect coverage due to preexisting conditions? http://bit.ly/35yMSQ[25]

Media or Public Relations

Tweets in which a Representative or Senator provided information about an upcoming media appearance.

> On Fox & Friends now talking about health care![26]
> On Rachel Maddow right after this commercial break. Tune in![27]

District or State

Tweets in which a Representative or Senator discussed a trip, visit, or event in a home district or state. Tweets might include invitations for Tweet recipients to attend town-hall meetings or events in the state or district.

> Reminder that I'm holding a health care town hall TOMORROW (Sept. 2) in the Rancho Buena Vista high school gym at 630 PM. #tcot[28]
> Awesome Jefferson parade. Passionate crowd. People calling for leadership.[29]

Official Congressional Action

Tweets in which a Representative or Senator described or recounted an official congressional action. For example, a Member might tweet about a roll call vote, or discuss participation in a committee hearing or recent trip abroad.

> Headed abroad to visit troops in theater.[30]
> Attended Top Secret briefing on Afghanistan. Situation deteriorating. Pentagon preparing to ask for more troops. Need focus on this problem.[31]

Personal

Tweets in which a Representative or Senator discussed events in his or her personal life or provided opinions concerning matters that were explicitly unrelated to work in Congress.

> While in St. Joseph I made a second stop at the Stetson outlet store to get a second pair of Levi's.[32]
> Quick visit w Fraser – world's cutest nephew. Starting to smile ....[33]

Campaign

Tweets in which a Representative or Senator included campaign-related material. These included calls for fundraising support, mentions of campaign-related events, or criticisms of campaign opponents.

> My campaign just released a web video to help spread our message. I hope you'll watch & share with your friends....[34]
> Thx to all those who have joined, sent shout outs, & supported my campaign so far. Help get the word out....[35]

Other

A catch-all category for Tweets that did not meet the definitional requirement of the other categories, or did not include enough information for a proper categorization.

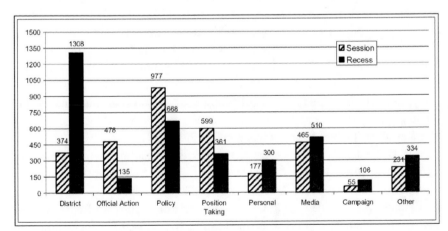

Source: CRS analysis of Twitter data for August and September 2009.

Figure 6. Member Tweets, by Category Including Session and Recess Comparison.

As shown in Figure 6, the most common Member tweets in session were "policy" tweets and during recess were "district" tweets. Policy tweets comprised 29% of in-session tweets and 18% of recess tweets and "district" tweets accounted for 11% of in-session tweets and 35% of recess tweets. The variance in "district" tweets may reflect the changing nature of Members' daily duties in session and during recess from legislating in Washington to representation in the district.

During session, "position taking," "media," and "official action" tweets were common, comprising 18%, 34%, and 14% of all tweets, respectively. With the exception of media tweets, such tweets were less common during recess. The three remaining types of tweets—"personal," "campaign," and "other" comprised approximately 5% of all tweets in session and 20% of all tweets during recess.

Technological innovations have altered traditional patterns of communication between Members of Congress and their constituents. However, at this time, Twitter largely facilitates a one-way transmission of information from Members to the public. Members use Twitter to convey information about their official actions, press appearances, or policy positions. Given the limited data available thus far, a two-way exchange of information or policy dialogue appears less frequent. Of the 7,078 tweets coded, only 261 (3.7%) were direct replies to other tweets.[38]

How Widely Are Member Tweets Being Followed?

The effectiveness of using Twitter to communicate information is partially dependent on the number of "followers" that have subscribed to an individual Twitter stream. The number of followers of any individual stream varies widely; a private citizen using Twitter only to communicate with his or her family might have only a handful of followers, whereas several contemporary celebrities currently have millions of followers.[39] Because the marginal cost of sending a Tweet to an additional follower is zero, there is little reason for a Member using Twitter to prefer fewer subscribers.

On December 30, 2009, data were collected on the number of subscribed followers for each Member of Congress with a registered Twitter account. In aggregate, Members had a total of 2,328,809 followers. The median Representative had 1,297 followers, with the most-followed Representative having more than 19,434 followers and the least-followed having 8 followers. In the Senate, the median Member had 3,536 followers, with the least-followed Senator having 216 followers, and the most-followed Senator having almost 1.7 million followers.[40]

Republican Members of the House of Representatives had more followers than their Democratic counterparts. The median Republican Representative had 1,563 followers, compared with 879 for the median Democratic Representative. For the Senate, the median Senate Democrat had slightly more followers than their Republican counterparts. The median Republican Senator had 3,216 followers, compared with 3,747 for the median Senate Democrat. The difference between House and Senate follower numbers likely reflects that most Senators represent larger constituencies than most Representatives, and arguably have greater national presence outside their districts.

CONCLUSION

The use of Twitter by Members of Congress is an evolving phenomenon. As Members continue to embrace new technologies, their use of Twitter and other forms of social media may increase. These mediums allow Members to communicate directly with constituents (and others) in a potentially interactive way that is not possible through mail or e-mail. For Members and their staff, the ability to collect and transmit real time information from constituents could be influential for policy or voting decisions.

End Notes

[1] Alfred A. Porro and Stuart A. Ascher, "The Case for the Congressional Franking Privilege," *University of Toledo Law Review*, vol. 5 (Winter 1974), pp. 280-281.

[2] Other studies have been conducted on the use of Twitter by Members of Congress. For example, see Jennifer Golbeck, Justin Grimes, and Anthony Rogers, "Twitter Use by the U.S. Congress," working paper, College Park, MD, 2009. [Hereafter, *Golbeck, Grimes, and Rogers, 2009*]. Goldbeck, Grimes, and Rogers collected a total of approximately 6,000 tweets for their analysis. A copy is available from CRS upon request. Also, see Mark Senak, "Twongress: The Power of Twitter in Congress," January 2010, http://www.eyeonfda.com/files/twongress-white-paper-final-1-14-10.pdf; Daniel de Vise, "Tweeting Their Own Horns," *The Washington Post*, September 20, 2009, p. A13; and University of Maryland, College Park, "UM Study Shows Congressional Use of Twitter Falls Short," press release, September 15, 2009, http://www.newsdesk.umd.edu/culture/release.cfm?articleID=1964.

[3] For journalistic accounts of the rise of electronic communications in Congress, see Elizabeth Brotherton, "A Different Kind of Revolution; Technology Redefines Constituent Outreach," *Roll Call*, September 10, 2007, p. 1; Amy Doolittle, "31 Days, 32 Million Messages," *Politico*, February 27, 2007, p. 1; Jonathan Kaplan, "2008 Candidates search Web for next new thing," *The Hill*, November 29, 2006, p. 6; David Haase, "Twitter: One More Medium, Much Shorter Messages," *Roll Call*, July 23, 2009, p. 4; and Daniel Newhauser, "Congress is All Atwitter," *Roll Call*, January 25, 2010, p. A-17.

[4] Chris Casey, *The Hill on the Net: Congress Enters the Information Age* (Chestnut Hill, MA: Academic Press, Inc., 1996), pp. 29-35.

[5] Data provide by the Office of the Chief Administrative Officer, House of Representatives.

[6] A survey of the YouTube Senate Hub homepage (http://www.youtube.com/user/senatehub) finds a large range in the number of views each video has received. Some videos have only a few dozen views while others have received tens of thousands of views.

[7] Data provided by the Office of the Chief Administrative Officer of the House of Representatives and the Office of the Secretary of the Senate. See also Kathy Goldschmidt and Leslie Ochreiter, *Communicating with Congress: How the Internet has Changed Citizen Identification*, Congressional Management Foundation, Washington, DC.

[8] This substantially differentiates electronic mail from franked mail, which does incur a marginal cost. See CRS Report RL34188, *Congressional Official Mail Costs*, by Matthew Eric Glassman.

[9] See CRS Report RL34274, *Franking Privilege: Historical Development and Options for Change*, by Matthew Eric Glassman.

[10] See Emily Yehle, "YouTube Gets No $, but Good PR," *Roll Call*, January 14, 2009, p. 4.

[11] For specific House and Senate policies, see U.S. Senate Internet Services Usage Rules and Policies, adopted September 19, 2009, available at http://www.senate.gov/usage/internet policy.htm; and House of Representatives Member's Handbook, Committee on House Administration, available at http://cha.house.gov/members_handbook.aspx.

[12] Twitter, "Where did Twitter Come From?" *About Twitter*, http://twitter.com/about. For more information about social networking see Danah M. Boyd and Nicole B. Ellison, "Social Networking Sites: Definition, History, and Scholarship," *Journal of Computer-Mediated Communication*, vol. 13, no. 1 (October 2007), pp. 210-230; and Lee Humphreys, "Mobile Social Networks and Social Practice: A Case Study of Dodgeball," *Journal of Computer-Mediated Communication*, vol. 13, no. 1 (October 2007), pp. 341-360.

[13] An RSS feed, which stands for Really Simple Syndication, is an opt-in service that allows users to receive targeted content from webpages, blogs, and online news sources. For more information, see Tom Barnes, "RSS: Marketing's Newest Communication Channel," *Journal of Website Promotion*, vol. 1, no. 4 (2005), pp. 15-30.

[14] U.S. Government Accountability Office, *Twitter*, http://twitter.com/usgao.

[15] Library of Congress, *Twitter*, http://twitter.com/librarycongress.

[16] U.S. Government Printing Office, *Twitter*, http://twitter.com/USGPO.

[17] Law Library of Congress, *Twitter*, http://twitter.com/LawLibCongress.

[18] House Dining Services, tweet, September 1, 2009, http://twitter.com/ushrcafes/status/36895 23683.

[19] See http://tweetcongress.org. Tweet Congress is a website that encourages more Members of Congress to use Twitter. The website tracks every Representative and Senator who uses Twitter, and reports their tweets in an ongoing stream.

[20] A previous CRS report analyzed two weeks of congressional Twitter use. See CRS Report R40823, *Social Networking and Constituent Communication: Member Use of Twitter During a Two-Week Period in the 111th Congress*, by Matthew Eric Glassman, Jacob R. Straus, and Colleen J. Shogan.

[21] These eight categories constitute one plausible way to examine the data collected from Twitter; other categories may also be defensible. These eight categories, however, are differentiable from each other, and capture all the tweets issued during this two-month time period.

[22] http://twitter.com, September 10, 2009.

[23] http://twitter.com, September 9, 2009.

[24] http://twitter.com, September 19, 2009.

[25] http://twitter.com, September 2, 2009.

[26] http://twitter.com, September 1, 2009.

[27] http://twitter.com, September 9, 2009.

[28] http://twitter.com, September 1, 2009.

[29] http://twitter.com, September 20, 2009.

[30] http://twitter.com, September 3, 2009.

[31] http://twitter.com, September 16, 2009.

[32] http://twitter.com, September 1, 2009.

[33] http://twitter.com, September 26, 2009.

[34] http://twitter.com, August 18, 2009.

[35] http://twitter.com, September 22, 2009.

[36] http://twitter.com, September 30, 2009.

[37] http://twitter.com, September 12, 2009.

[38] A different coding schema with additional categories produces slightly different results. Golbeck, Grimes, and Rogers used a nine-category coding scheme with categories including direct communication, personal messages, activities, information, requesting action, fundraising, and unknown. They found that the majority of tweets were information tweets (53%), followed by location or activity tweets (27%), and constituent (or outside Congress) communications (7%). *Golbeck, Grimes, and Rogers, 2009*, p. 4.

[39] Many Internet sites have been developed to rank Twitter users by their number of followers. For example, see http://twittercounter.com/pages/100 and http://twitterholic.com/. Each of these websites list the top Twitter user as having approximately 3.5 million followers.

[40] The median number of followers for Members of Congress was used instead of the mean because of an outlier in the dataset. One Member of Congress has more than 1.2 million followers. Inclusion of this data point in the calculation of the mean provides an unrealistic average of followers for all Members using Twitter.

INDEX